Vagabonds of

The Campaign of a French cruiser

Maurice Larrouy

(Translator: Randolph Silliman Bourne)

Alpha Editions

This edition published in 2024

ISBN : 9789362096272

Design and Setting By
Alpha Editions
www.alphaedis.com
Email - info@alphaedis.com

As per information held with us this book is in Public Domain.
This book is a reproduction of an important historical work. Alpha Editions uses the best technology to reproduce historical work in the same manner it was first published to preserve its original nature. Any marks or number seen are left intentionally to preserve its true form.

Contents

PART I THE AWAKENING OF THE CRUISER...................- 1 -
PART II IN THE ADRIATIC..- 9 -
PART III IN THE IONIAN SEA...- 70 -

PART I
THE AWAKENING OF THE CRUISER

From Paris to Toulon, end of July, 1914.

FROM the corridor I watch through the windows the swift receding of Paris. In this express-train, the last to run according to the normal schedule, are numerous naval officers en route for Toulon. Some have broken their brief vacations; almost all are returning on leaves of absence from their studies. The call of our country sends us towards the sea, that field of battle which we have chosen. To the French Navy belongs the "honor" of the Mediterranean, and our fleet is at its summit of preparedness. We know that the decisive duel will be fought in the fields of Flanders or on the slopes of the Vosges. But our effort will not be useless. We have only one fear—that we shall arrive too late, and miss that battle which our imaginations have pictured without actually believing.

Dijon, Lyons, Valence, Marseilles. I have just left a Paris full of excitement, where life is of so poignant a sweetness that the people are eager to defend the happiness they possess in such abundance. I am traveling through our smilingFrance. How many times, as I have passed from one seaport to another, on my way from a Chinese to an Atlantic cruise, have I not understood the envy which is directed towards her! How could our neighbors help casting towards this delightful land the glances of beasts of prey! Now they have spread out their claws, and hurled at her a cry of war. France has drawn herself erect. Everywhere squads of sentinels are guarding the roadways, the crossings, the stations, all the nerve-centers of mobilization. Into the eyes of the French people these last few days has come a magnificent expression; a new visage, which our race has put on as if for a fête, gives a family likeness to all its members. The foster-mother of children like these is no moribund being such as the Germans think they will succeed in doing away with. She has just felt again the vivid sense of her duty, and the heirs of her wonderful past draw from her strength attitudes so natural that they are not even astonished at them. This astonishment they leave to the rest of the world.

Dijon, Lyons, Valence, Marseilles, Naguére. I amuse myself with observing the various types and accents of the provinces. To-day everyone speaks the same language, has the same expression; in every breast is the same heart. I know that in the West, in the regions I have not traveled through, Gascons, Normans, and Picardsare feeling and acting alike. Among these troops assembled on the platforms of the stations, in the sleeping cottages of remote countrysides, in the towns past which glides our flashing train, there is only one dream. This dream I know, for it is my own:

"What post does France give me for the great combat? Wherever it may be, whether I fall, or whether I survive, it will be well."

Toulon, 1 August.

Alas! Several hours have passed, and I find that all is not well. The vessels of the "naval army" have their staffs of officers completed, and from hour to hour await the order to put to sea. I was assigned to the *Waldeck-Rousseau*. At another time I should have been proud to be a part of this splendid vessel. But she is not prepared to leave port. In an accident at sea some months ago, she ripped herself open on the shoals of the Gulf of Juan. The healing of great ships is a tedious affair, and in a repair basin the engineers are still treating her gaping wounds. In reply to my anxious questions, I am told:

"The workmen are busy on her day and night. In six weeks she will take the water again."

Six weeks! And the other night on the train I saw myself already at sea, my vessel en route for her assigned zone. And now I must be satisfied with a cruiser that will not stir for six weeks!

[4]*2 August.*

We lived in an atmosphere heated by the sun of Provence. Arriving from Paris as I did, I was questioned. Circles formed, strangers consulted me. In vain did I relate what I had seen in the North, describe my journey on the railway; these listeners only half believed me. In the climate of Provence care disappears; my questioners shook their heads. One regretted his ruined vacation; another doubted my testimony; some of them invoked the prudence of the Powers, and concluded:

"Everything will end in a 'Congress of Algeciras.'"

Far removed from the vivid Parisian energy, I felt myself overcome by the enervation of Provence. The whole drama of the week took on the guise of nightmare. I was annoyed that the great convulsion, ordered by Fate, seemed once more delayed by man. I reproached my prudent friends for not taking their part in it. Before them the curtain of an epic drama was already rising, and they were not hailing with enthusiastic acclaim the opening of the spectacle. Their mediocre souls were merely taking up again the thread of their daily preoccupations!

Towards two o'clock I cross the threshold of the arsenal gate, to pay the *Waldeck-Rousseau* my visit of embarkation. The sky is pouringdown an avalanche of dusty heat. In such an oven no one can think vigorously. Sprawled against the walls, the arsenal workers are mopping their faces and chests, and, at the end of their tether, are drinking greedily at the roadside bars. Several officers, handkerchiefs in hand, are walking along the rows of plane-trees.

The commander of the *Waldeck-Rousseau* receives me:

"You are in luck," he says. "All the officers who arrive at the port ask for the *Waldeck-Rousseau*."

He guesses the question I dare not utter.

"The engineers are counting on six weeks.... Let us hope nothing decisive happens at sea ... in case events are so precipitate...."

Thinking over these words, I return to the gate of the arsenal. It is getting on towards five o'clock. The flame and shimmer of the afternoon light are marvelous. The Pharon, a mirror of stone, reflects the dazzling violet rays. It is the hottest part of the day. After this will follow cooling breezes. In front of the Missiessy gate mothers and wives crouch on the sidewalk, awaiting their sailors, who come out of the arsenal raising clouds of dust. A beverage-vender calls his wares in a nasal voice; several barkers offer for ten centimes a hundred attractions in the way of café-concerts; the tramcars, caparisoned in dust, go by in a torrid blast. It is so warm, theboulevard is so torpid, that I cannot think, and have but one swift desire—to change my stifling uniform for a more comfortable suit, and on a terrace to sip some cooling drink.

Suddenly, smothered by the distance and the heavy air, a dull cannon shot strikes into the fringe of my reverie. I fear I have heard amiss. I wait motionless, my whole body concentrated in my hearing. The boulevard seems petrified. With a brusque jamming on of brakes, the tramcars grind along the track; the windows bristle with anxious faces. The women squatting on the sidewalk silently rise; barkers and passers-by forget to live; everyone, in the posture in which the vague shot has surprised him, listens to the dramatic silence. All the noises of the city, the deepest as well as the shrillest, vanish into nothingness to leave room for the one sound that has significance. In a sort of religious atmosphere the second shot booms and rolls, sonorous, the master of Space.... At length the third dies away, the third voice of a France who is placing herself on guard.

At the same time, over the deserted roadway, the trumpets sound from the barracks. Listen to those majestic singing tones, which bring tears to the driest eyelids! It is the call of France! Drawn up under the great trees a whole wan city salutes two little soldiers who swell their cheeks upon the shining trumpets. They are muchaffected, these two little soldiers in fatigue uniform; their step is hesitant, and their breath breaks. But their eyes are sparkling, each measure brings new vigor to their step, they find the theme again, and without taking breath they sound the "générale" out to the suburbs, to the slopes of the Pharon, to the roads of the countryside roundabout. They are the heralds of their country.

At this instant all over this land the same trumpet is being blown. It has found me in a warm and fragrant province, but everywhere millions of reapers, with suspended sickles, are listening to the same notes flung out over oceans of grain. Mountains and valleys give back its echo to the huts of cattlemen and shepherds, and the silent waters of the rivers quiver as they receive its melody. For the first time in the course of the centuries the race of France is listening at the same instant to a voice which orders her to face towards a common point. Stirred by a great hope, her hearts are celebrating together this first communion of heroism.

Fortune compels me to wait six weeks before playing my rôle. My weapon of war is not yet ready. I can only admire, as a spectator, deeds in which I have no share.

In the streets leading to the harbor, the heart of Toulon, swarm crowds of people. I am not acquainted with these figures that slip along besideme, but I recognize them all. Marines from Brittany, blue-eyed, with swinging step, white-coiffed wives on their arms; sailors of Provence, brown and eloquent; thick-set Basques and fair Flemings—all these men whom I have commanded, managed, loved, hasten along their way. A kind of enchantment dilates their eyes, a sort of innocent ecstasy. They go gaily towards the sea and the combat, towards their constant mistress and their unknown bride. Already the squadrons have steam up; a forest of stacks vomit streamers of smoke which portend adventurous cruises. They get under weigh to-night; perhaps to-morrow the great adventure will occur. The sides of the ironclads and cruisers in the roadstead let loose a flock of boats and launches to seek on the quay their loads of brave marines.

Around the approaches to the wharves it is impossible to move. There is a suppressed shuffling of feet; only jackets and uniforms can get through to the boats. I slip in. On the sidewalk a Breton woman is weeping softly into the corner of her apron; her four little children, lost in the forest of legs, press round her skirt, clutching the cloth with their fingers; heads turned upward, they watch through great limpid eyes the endless flow of people. Each step reveals a similar scene; women clasp for the last time their beloved son, lover, or husband; their frail arms cannot let himgo, and their tongues are stammering inexpressible things. Yet, as I listen, I hear in all this chorus of despair not a single word of revolt. These women comprehend everything. They nod their heads approvingly at the words of those who are leaving them. Their last kiss holds even a smile, a heavenly smile, which the fighting man is to carry with him on the sea, and recall at the instant of death. But when the sailor has disappeared toward the boats, the smile slowly fades; the women bite their lips, their faces grow distorted, and the tears, more sublime for having been held back so long, trickle through lids which for many months will not cease to weep.

As becomes naval tragedies, the farewell took place in a splendid setting. The twilight was glorious with an incomparable splendor of sky, and the purple evening seemed to vibrate in unison with the city. On the edge of the quay, between the boats and the crowd, I could watch the faces, both of those who had to stay behind, and of those who were leaving. As long as the sailors were forcing their way along between those parting embraces and the boats, they were pale beneath their tan, and only with difficulty restrained their sobs. But hardly had they jumped to the benches of the launches, hardly had their comrades greeted them with hearty blows on shoulders and hips, when their color returned, their mouths let forth sonorous pleasantries, andthey thought no more of anything but the sea and the adventure.

At my feet hundreds of sailors are laughing and singing; they intoxicate themselves with anticipation in order not to betray their tenderness and their grief. On the quay, overshadowing this gayety, stands a forlorn crowd; those in front smile vaguely, but those behind are silently choking back their tears. And over there in the gold-flaked roadstead, the gray ships sparkle in the setting sun. All faces turn towards them. They are the geniuses of the moment. Entrusted with a portion of the honor of France, they await their orders. Before their prows, the country has swung open the gates of glory. Their guns and their sailors are made of the same steel.

3 August.

In the morning I went with some friends to the top of Cape Capet to see the departure of the "naval army."

On the *Courbet*, flagship of the commander-in-chief, the admirals had assembled in a night council of war. A few hours later, in the deep silence of the blue morning, the squadrons began to move. One after another, they took position and formed before our eyes; we heard the faint sound of orders. On the heavy water the ships moved without an eddy; squat, slender, or graceful, battleships, cruisers, or torpedo-boats fell into well-orderedformations, and quietly took their proper distances and intervals. They reminded one of ancient gladiators stripped naked for the combat. During these last days they had sent back to the land-stores all the superfluities of peace; they had kept only the bare necessities in rigging and boats, and the paint on their steel sides had disappeared under the hand of the scraper.

Their only ornament is the curling smoke which rises through the still air and mingles on high in an immense cloud modeled by the faint breeze. Their only paint is the light flashing on port-holes and brass. Their only finery, the guns, well-cleared, with mouths pointing out to sea. They are beautiful and they are invincible. Designed for battle and the chase, they push their bows through the water they know so well, on their way to carry to enemy shores the frontier of France. At the hour when human beings are still asleep, they go to take possession of the field of battle.

Their task is various and hard, and without any doubt destined to remain unappreciated. On the sea the paths are innumerable, and the legends of the sea tell of many a patient cruiser that has rarely been rewarded by a battle.

The transports have to carry to France our troops from North Africa. To the "naval army" belongs the duty of protecting these lives. No one can tell whether or not this enterprise willbe successful. Let a single transport fail the summons, and a deluge of sarcasm will fall upon the fleet of war! Let sharpshooters and Algerian cavalry within fifteen days show their mettle in the valleys of the Vosges, and who will give thanks to those who had protected their dangerous voyage? No matter! France has distributed the tasks among her children. To the fighters on the frontier falls the honor of crushing the Germans; to the sailors, the silent guard of the sea.

Perhaps, however, these too will not be denied the glory of battle. At the foot of the Adriatic, Austria maintains a fleet that without doubt will try to rob us of our empire of the Mediterranean. To release her shores she will offer us a naval engagement. The fleet of France will prove itself no less worthy than the army; and its deeds, less decisive than those of Alsace and of Flanders, will yet prove that the flag which flaps at the stern of her ships is without stain.

Au Revoir!

Eve of departure, 5 September.

The crew and staff of the *Waldeck-Rousseau* are stirring to snatch a day, an hour, from the delay of her departure; already we have gained two weeks.

Stretched on its granite rests, the cruiser resembles some metal giant harnessed with machinery. With a great pounding of hammers,the cohorts of expert workmen are putting life into the great hull. Each day the Depot sends us marine reservists, with instructions as to the posts and offices where they are to labor and to fight. A thousand men are assembled now, and the engineers have given the ship over to us.

Shining and new she floats. Like a thoroughbred that after a sickness breaks her own record, the good cruiser has gained some tenths of a mile on her old speed. The steam runs freely in her arteries, the electricity through her nerves. From bow to stern a hundred and fifty meters of steel are aquiver. Off the Hyeres Islands, on a fine August day, the voice of her guns, so many months silenced, resounds again in celebration of her recovery. Woe to anyone who passes within ten kilometers of our cannon!

From hour to hour, little by little, officers and men extend their control of the vessel, and get better acquainted with her mazes. As their skill becomes surer, they adapt themselves to the particular moods of the ship, and to her caprices, which can only be mastered with prudence and with affection.

Our crew, an amorphous crowd collected at random from the four quarters of France, had lost that sense of discipline and responsibility which the humblest of sailors should have. We have had to drill them, direct their discordant forces, and make them a living being animatedby a will. Each one in his place now applies his intelligence and his strength to his special task, and tries to get himself into trim. Time presses. In a few days we have put new life into the great torpid cruiser. After a few hours we shall depart, nor shall we cut the figure of poor relations or of cripples in the "naval army."

Thank heaven, the decisive action has held off. We dread the telegram announcing an encounter of the fleets; but it has not yet come. Opening the chapter of Mediterranean events, the *Breslau* and the *Goeben*, German cruisers, have attacked Algerian ports, and fled towards the Dardanelles, where a miracle has turned them into Turks. Here is game for a later time. In the middle of August the French navy has sunk the *Zepta*, a small Austrian cruiser. But that's a minor affair. We shall arrive in time.

On certain evenings we go to sleep on land. Friend of those who frequent her, the sea is execrated by the women who live on her shores; their mourning is harsh and bitter. War adds tenfold to their anxieties. Our comrades who left at the beginning of August suffered an uprooting that was short and sharp. We, who have remained too long, run the gamut of anxious concern. For those men from my cruiser who meet feminine affection on shore, each moment holds an unknown torture. Between a sob and a caresspasses the phantom of naval hecatombs. Beneath his lowered eyelids the sailor sees his future glory, but the arms clasped about his breast are an embrace of despair. A sunset, a walk between dusty hedges or over fragrant grass—everything suggests agitation and dread. Eye and ear acquire a mysterious perceptivity. One longs to retain, like a viaticum, the voices of loved ones in their most inconsequential inflections. We can bid farewell to France, for the treasures of our hearts have been wrung dry.

To this feeling the sadness of the news from the front adds poignancy. When in the morning the officers study the map of operations, brought up to date according to the communiqué, a profound silence falls over the salon of the

Waldeck-Rousseau. We cannot believe this sweep over Belgium, this tidal wave over the French provinces. We wish to depart, to do no matter what, to work, to die. Under our feet the cruiser trembles, our own child, our friend, our master. Each hour of delay irritates us. We are indifferent about the road to victory. Painful and tragic as it is, all Frenchmen accept it, and the sailors about to leave cherish no other thought. The other day, while a crew of gunners were loading shells charged with melinite, I overheard this exclamation from a man whose brawny arms held a yellow projectile:

"Gawd! Why don't they just use shells stuffed with sawdust? It wouldn't take any more than that to give them theirs!"

I doubt if this war will be won in so childish a manner. But it is pleasant for an officer to command such children.

PART II
IN THE ADRIATIC

Adriatic Sea, 25 September.

THE ships keep shelter in Pola and Cattaro, and will not come out! There is nothing Austrian in sight except the names on the maps and the silent coasts. We continue, however, to sail along the shore, we brave their submarines, their mines, their torpedo-boats. Like the knights of the Crusades challenging their adversaries, we go to offer ourselves to their attack. But they do not issue forth.

Like a great army corps that waits the engagement, the armored squadrons run the barrage of Otranto. They are the lions of our naval menagerie. Claws sheathed, jaws closed, they strain their ears for the call of the cruisers.... In small groups the torpedo-destroyers circle round them, sweeping the road where the great beasts of battle are about to pass, and watching to see that no submarine is prowling on the path.

Further north on the skirts of the Adriatic great-lunged battleships are holding the jungle. The cruisers know no rest; they pursue their anxious watch along the outposts, traversing thewaves and piercing the sky. Upon their observations, in sun and shadow, depends the safety of the great battleships. Theirs is the joy of spying the enemy upon the horizon, of rushing forward, of receiving the first shots and launching the first shells, of so calculating the retreat as to draw the enemy within range of the battleships' guns.

We are three brothers—the *Ernest Renan*, the *Edgar Quinet*, are as beautiful and majestic as the *Waldeck-Rousseau*. Their six stacks belch forth the same clouds. Engaged in the same work, all are acquainted with the same fatigue. Older and less sturdy, the *Gambetta*, the *Ferry*, the *Hugo*, and the *Michelet* have the same tasks. Their family is known by its four smokestacks.

From Otranto to Fano, and along its whole shadowy line, the seven cruisers blockade the Adriatic at the end of which the Austrians are entrenched. From the summit of the bridge one can see for ten miles; that is why we navigate at twenty miles' distance, on circuits of short circumference, ever the same. The cruisers never sight each other, but each knows that below the horizon a brother ship is within reach and on guard. Sometimes the ceaseless rhythm of their march brings them to the confines of their "beat," and they sight each others' masts glistening on the horizon like the bayonets of a double sentry. Then both tack about, and go their opposite directions; the masts sink out of sight, the smokedrifts away, and nothing is left but a solitary vigil on a deserted sea.

Since our departure from Toulon the *Waldeck-Rousseau* has been in constant motion. In the waste of waters the clamors of the world are stilled. We have commenced the pilgrimage known to so many generations of sailors. At a venture we halt some small game—packet-boats, three-masted schooners, or steamers, which submit to our examination. They bring us a faint echo of human affairs—Italians, Greeks, or Spaniards—and are fraught with I know not what continental aroma. We send these timid travelers on their voyage; their examination is but play; the important affair lies up there at Pola or Cattaro. Every week after coaling—which we do at sea—we go and shake our fists at the enemy, crying shame upon him in his retreat and challenging him to an encounter. Many times already we have gone up there in the night; in the daytime we have circled about Lissa, the Dalmatian Isles, and even further still. Far behind us the battleships follow, alert for the signal—"Enemy in sight!" But our guns are leveled in vain; in vain our eyes face the tracery of sun and shadow. Nothing appears within our range except the motionless shores, the slumbering isles—never a quarry.

This disappointment does not slacken our vigilance. In times of peace a single lieutenant, aided by an ensign, suffices for the many duties involved in managing a ship. Whether it has to do with observing the heavens, avoiding collisions, or coordinating the movements of many hundreds of sailors, during his four hours' command he can easily attend to and handle it all.

Those times are no more. War puts a tenfold burden upon the cruiser without adding to its staff of officers. For now the ship is at once an organ of navigation and an instrument of battle. This duality of function demands at every moment two directing heads; the first continues to direct the watch, the second assumes responsibility for the lookout, defense, and battle. On the *Waldeck* we have only six lieutenants; so we form three crews of two each, who relieve one another on the bridge in an endless round, by day and night, in all weathers. One of them looks after the route, the crew and the signals from the shores; the other keeps his eye upon the sea and is ready at any moment to let loose the guns. My rank of seniority gives me the second rôle.

Throughout the rest of the war, whether it be short or long, my mate and I are destined to the same changes of fortune. He must have my confidence, and I his. These things are not uttered. But they are implicit in our handshake at the moment when we take the watch and assume the precious charge of the ship for our four-hour period.

He is a Fleming, I am Latin. This difference extends even to our ways of thinking, and lends piquancy to our two daily meetings. As we lean on the bridge rail, he at port and I at starboard, we watch the sea with equal vigilance. But in our secret souls move thoughts which have nothing to do with our profession. This is one of the privileges of men of action. They can surrender themselves wholly to their task without ceasing to dream of a thousand things. My comrade and I talk in low voices. The war, Germany, the future, everything comes up in these murmured conversations. We do not believe in keeping silent, for our motionless position is likely to bury us in a dangerous torpor. As our eyes search space, we passionately discuss the great drama, and we never agree. But if, in the treacherous night, a shadow appears, or a suspicious shape, suddenly we are one. Each performs instantly the necessary rites; one commands the helm and the machinery, the other directs the primers and gunners. The two of us in the darkness cooperate perfectly.

And then a few minutes later the scare is over. The gunners resume their posts, the primers unprime the guns. We two officers—one on the port, the other on the starboard—continue our vigil and our whispered talk.

Adriatic Sea, 27 September.

Three English cruisers—the *Cressy*, the *Hogue* and the *Aboukir*—have just found their last resting-place in the North Sea. Still intact, but bearing in their sides torpedo-wounds, they have slipped into their winding-sheet of seaweed, where the skeletons of vessels sunk in ancient wars await them. The sea-water, that patient embalmer, will reclothe their keels with a shroud of rust and lime. On bright days, when the sun shines on the still sea, they will see the shadows of living vessels pass overhead. They will be caressed by the ripple from those screws, and their petrified hulks will quiver with pleasure. During the tedious hours of the lookout, I have been meditating upon the wireless messages which announced the death of the *Cressy*, the *Hogue*, and the *Aboukir*. That same tragedy may cut short the very phrases which I am commencing to unite. I imagine the whole scene, I recreate it. I have sailed the North Sea, I have lived two years in a submarine, and I am at war now on a cruiser.

I see three ships, somber and silent like ourselves, following the course laid down by the Admiral. North and south, other patrol vessels are traversing the appointed routes. While the soldiers of France and the children of England sleep, the sailors are keeping watch on the sea, that no one may force the barriers of their countries.But the sea is illimitable, the cruisers are few and far between, and cannot lend each other aid. For this the sailor must make up in toil and weariness; he takes less sleep, he watches unceasingly, he is always cold, he never touches land. Up there, just as in the Adriatic, he mounts his guard, longing with all his heart for an adventure.

Thus sailed the *Cressy*, the *Hogue*, and the *Aboukir*, how many days I do not know. But I do know the vigilance, the labor, the self-sacrifice of their crews. More than all the others, they offered their souls to the service of victory— these sailors whose ships are decorated with the famous names of English victories. These three noble names, did they not foretell a new harvest of laurels? Did they not symbolize a return to more fraternal policies, which dedicated to the service of France these namesakes of French defeats? English officers and sailors, with the clear instinct of men participating in great deeds, should offer France, in a single victory over our common enemies, a recompense for these three disasters England had inflicted upon her!

This night passed like all the others. Along the horizon were trails of gray light. The rolling sea emerged from the chaos of dawn, and the lookouts, with heavy heads and quivering eyelids, scanned for the thousandth time the troubled awakening of the North Sea. They saw nothing. Perhaps one of them had descried a streak of foam whiter and clearer than the rest, and quickly raised his glass to his eyes. But the streak of foam had already been covered again, and he dropped the glass which had not revealed the periscope. The three cruisers pursued their way amid the ridges of foam, one of which, though they were unaware of it, meant death to them.

A shock went through the first ship. The sailors on deck thought there had occurred an accident to the machinery; those below thought that a gun had been fired.... Everyone listened. Under the brave fellows' feet the ship turned, lazily at first, while the waves boiled impatiently about her. Then they understood, all of them; they knew that death was near. Before they sank into the sailors' grave, they looked again for the enemy who had destroyed them without granting them the joy of battle. Their staring eyes fell upon their comrade of the patrol, and filled with fear, for the *Aboukir* was lurching too. Both had been stung to death by the stealthy advance of the submarine vipers. Generous still in their very death-agony, the two wounded ships hoisted warning signals, that their comrade might evade the deadly track. But she, as generous in her pity, raced to save the lives of the sailors in the engulfing waters. She too received her mortal wound, without being able to fire a single gun, although, clearer-sighted in the face of death, she was able to discern the submarine under its white streak of water.

As the chill of the hemlock poison rises to the heart, the water rose in the three ships. The boilers choked with it, the machinery was drowned; one by one the watertight compartments, exploded by the pressure of the waves, burst with the noise of thunder. The electricity failed everywhere at once, and the sea became a tomb where men struggled and were buffeted by the waves. On the deck, drawn up in line, the crews gazed straight into their doom. The triple choir raised a hymn which they had learned on their English Sabbaths, and they sank to meet their God.

Farewell, sailors of the three cruisers, fallen perhaps through the same fate that is in store for our Adriatic cruisers! Your anguish, your vigils, your last thoughts, we feel here on the *Waldeck-Rousseau*. Your end was noble, even if no one around me envies it. For we pray the God of Battles, if he sends us death, that we may at least exact a heavy toll from our enemies!

Strait of Otranto, 8 October.

How can one describe the atmosphere of the Adriatic? For that marvel our most delicate adjectives are inadequate. It is more than diaphanous, better than translucent; it dreams. It seems to exist only to contain pure color.

How many times has this immaterial air deceived the officer of the watch! How many miles away is a certain steamer? In how many hours shall we skirt the island that rises amid the clouds?

Formerly we solved these problems without thought, for our eyes had learned to gauge the density of the air and its deceptions. The Adriatic atmosphere has lowered our conceit. Skies or sails, lighthouse or shore, each object is always further off than we suppose. Prudent now, we hesitate to say whether Corfu is thirty miles away, or that this pale line of the Otranto coast is not a cloud resting on the water. We are not wrong to mistrust ourselves. Corfu is fifty miles away, and this imagined cloud is the coast of Italy.

The officers on the bridge struggle with these illusions. The sea itself multiplies their difficulties. Formerly the sailor dreaded only what moved above the surface of the sea. He noticed at almost any distance traces of smoke, indistinct masts, and all the signs by which a ship reveals her presence. But the sailors of to-day level their gaze upon that surface which was once so innocent.... Between two crests floats a dark speck.... Is it not a mine charged with explosives? Those shining lines, like the trail of a snail, are they not the oily tracks of a submarine lying in wait for us?

But sailors learn secrets. Formerly, they contemplated the waves and ripples carelessly, as queer old comrades whose every mood one pardoned. But now they keep them under a stern inflexible eye. The play of a wave, the alternate strips of light, the shadows of a cloud—we grapple with everything, and never relax our vigilance. For everything is illusion.

The lookout wavers between a fear of being ridiculed and a fear of having seen amiss. There is never a day that some wireless message does not come from one of our sentinels of the sea, telling the "naval army" that a submarine is in sight. From Saint Maure to Lissa, from Tarento to Corfu, all the French ships are anxious about the outcome of this encounter, and hope that the comrade engaged will be victorious. Minutes slip away, we imagine the whole drama; a noble envy stirs every heart. And then the second message comes over the sea. "It was not a submarine!" it declares. Then the Adriatic and the Ionian Sea resound with a burst of mocking laughter, one of those bursts of laughter which only the descendants of the Gauls know how to give.

Tragedy, nevertheless, comes close on laughter. From the bridge the officer of the watch has seen something, two or three miles away, that is not quite the color of its surroundings. He fastens his glass on this dark or light speck, which moves slowly like a periscope on the lookout.... The thing disappears and reappears, like a periscope which is taking its bearings, ordering its course, and waiting.... The officer's heart leaps. His orders start the engines, direct the pilot, send the gunners to their guns. His body is tense with joy, his eyes shine; on the bridge, at the port-holes, officers and sailors follow the alarm with excited interest, and gaze out at the suspicious speck in the distance. Everyone envies the comrades who have charge of the ship at this brave moment, the gunners and steersmen who will pit their wits against the submarine. A sort of joyful anguish grips their hearts, for it is war to the death, and perhaps the torpedo is already launched and making straight for the keel. We fairly suffocate with excitement.

But some more experienced eye has made out the shape. "It's a bit of wood!" murmurs a top-man.... "No, it's a bottle!" whispers a gunner. Each one gives his opinion. "It's a seagull!" "It's the branch of a tree!" "It's a broom-handle!" "It's a box of preserves!" The uproar increases and rises to the officer on the bridge, who wipes his glass in order to see better. He is still expectant; he curses this encounter a thousand times. He is responsible for the boat and for all these laughing sailors. Torn between derision and danger, he remains prudent, and makes for the dangerous object, with the order to open fire still on the tip of his tongue.

Suddenly, when we are eight hundred or a thousand meters away, he takes a few nervous steps, countermands the alarm, orders the engines to slow down, and turns his eyes away from the preserve-box, the branch, the bottle, whatever it may be. The ship shoots by at a short distance. The jokers in the crew salute the innocent waif that floats past and disappears.... Unless it be a gull, busy with its bath; in which case it dives, preens its feathers, dives again, without bothering about the ship, or her officer on the bridge. Between its plunges, sunk up to its breast in the water, it rides past the flying steel monster with a mocking "Kwang! Kwang!"

At the end of his watch, the officer goes below to the ward-room where he is received with mocking laughter. These sorry jokes he scorns as a stoic should. He knows that the next night or to-morrow, at any moment, his comrades are as likely to make a mistake as he. We had all rather see a periscope than seagulls or branches. In the North Sea the *Cressy*, the *Hogue* and the *Aboukir* had seen gulls and branches a thousand times. The day they sighted nothing they went to their doom.

Adriatic Sea, 15 October.

The Adriatic is our private estate. The cruisers make use of it as if Austria did not exist. They ascend it, circle about, stop in frontof the islands, challenge the coasts, without a single visible enemy's attacking them. Doubtless the submarines come out daily from Cattaro in quest of the prize booty that our vessels would make. But either chance or our vigilance has prevented the disaster. We watch, we are worn out; nothing happens. Sometimes in the West, low on the water, trails the Italian coast; smoke floats over Otranto or Brindisi; for forty days this is all we have known of human activity. The lighthouse of Santa Marin of Leuca marks the uttermost point of Latin soil; it is a desolate object, like a pale needle stuck into the blue air. By night, its light falls on the veils of the horizon. It is one of the lonely friends of our solitude.

Towards the eastern coasts other friends watch our passage—the gaunt peaks of Albania or Epirus, or even the Ionian Archipelago, that delicate jewel of stone. Albania and Epirus! Famous but sinister names! Wherever Islam rules dwells devastation. The bases of the mountains are buried in the sea, and they look colossal; death lives on their gray slopes. A warm sun, however, shines on them, and busy hands may be tending vineyards and olive orchards. Yet one sees only masses of rocks, and the scars of mountain-streams. Here and there a bald yellowish circle stains the mass of stone. In that spot flourished in former times an Albanian or Epirote village. Fire destroyed it, and the fury of menhas left it only a charred waste. A dizzy silence comes from these mountains. It falls and rolls over the blue water, so hard a blue one thinks a hammer might strike sparks from it. No one lives in these somber regions. Along the bays and inlets barks with Levantine sails scud before the wind, passing by in all possible haste. These barks carry mountaineers crowded in their holds like sheep in a pen. In these brigand realms life is so unsafe that even the brigands themselves prefer the hazards of the sea to journeys by land.

Our cruiser halts these tiny boats. Then the human cargo bursts out from the hold, and their distress shows that they think their last hour has come. Clothed in sheepskins, armed with daggers and pistols, these rascals conceal in their hearts a world of unknown crime; every time they find it profitable they are ready to massacre and betray. Their dark minds do not know who we are nor why we have come. We can only be executioners, equipped with irresistible weapons.

The visiting officer reassures them, of course, with his gestures. The passengers remain suspicious; their keen eyes watch him as he points to the holds and orders their contents turned out. The bullies understand; we are robbers and will let their lives go in exchange for their merchandise. Pell-mell they throw out their figs, their bundles of dried fish, their little sacks of corn—wretched food of wretchedbeings. They spread them out at the foot of this plunderer in a lace-covered uniform. Their broken language and raised hands call Christ to witness, or Allah, or even the Demons of the caves, that nothing further of value is left in the hold. The officer turns the sacks over, opens some, for fear that cans of essence or cases of explosives have been the object of this furtive journey to Cattaro or Pola. His foraging fingers encounter nothing but figs or herrings, which leave on his finger-nails a faint spicy smell. Carelessly he wipes off with his handkerchief the mixed fragments of fruit sugar. With a severe glance he makes a last inspection of the boat. The good bandits relapse into disquietude. They don't understand; what does he want of them? One of them speaks, and at once their faces clear up. It is gold he demands, good sterling coin, an easy ransom to carry. The richer ones extract from their belts some pieces from the Balkan States, much worn and effaced; the poor ones spread out on their palms some sous and centimes, so bent and filed they are good only for jacket-buttons for our sailors. An old bashi-bazouk, white around the temples and at the ends of his mustache, has not a single good coin; crouched on the deck, he tells over a blackened rosary and from his god begs absolution for past sins. The others plead; the women kiss the hands and knees of the uniformed stranger; the children cry bitterly. The visiting officer embarks majestically in his long-boat, and makes a gesture of disdain that sends all this misery on its way again. The pilot hoists the sail, the rich man pockets his piasters and the beggar his coppers, the bashi-bazouk his prayers, the women their kisses, and the children their tears. The sheet swells, and the bark passes below the cruiser, whose crew smile indulgently, while our Albanians and Epirotes, seated on their hatches, understand nothing whatever.

On other days our police duty takes us further south. Steamers and sailing vessels frequent the approaches to Corfu, and our visits are more careful and more profitable. The shores have lost their gloomy appearance; black herds are pasturing on the hills; each slope is checkered in squares of olive orchards and clusters of vineyard; in little well-sheltered coves four white houses are grouped round a ruined mosque.

On the edge of the water, overhanging a harbor, rises the castle of some erstwhile pasha. This castle is round, copper-colored, classic in design, beautifully situated. The blue water reflects its pale image, and we often slow down for the mere pleasure of admiring it. Victor Hugo would have loved this stronghold, whence pirates used to surge forth, and the village where the booty was brought together; his lines would have celebrated the pasha-corsair, the beauty of his odalisks, and the romance of their jeweled retreat. These lovely walls, however, conceal tragedies of Islam. They brood over the sea paths, and their silence is that of a beaten vulture. I prefer to forget that sinister grandeur. I prefer this empty silhouette, artistically placed here in a happy setting for the brief delectation of a few passing sailors. These are empty pleasures, perhaps, but we have no others.

Perfect hours await us at sea, off Corfu, Paxo and Cephalonia. When the twilight unfolds its pageant of air and light, we get a sense of joy and confidence that sustains us in our exile. The sun sinks in a procession of purple clouds, shading away to a faint heliotrope in the sky overhead. From mid-heaven hang sheafs of eglantine and geranium, beneath which blossom red carnations, tulips and poppies. The sun feeds all this floral fire. Under the iridescent play of color the sea has disappeared. Its liquid surface has merged with the luminous air, and the cruiser, rose-colored, moves through myriad rainbows.

Everything about the suspended ship is changed to silence and fantasy. The shadows of twilight succeed the colors that glow and disappear. Air and sun create marvels that are not of our world. The light falls on us like a blessing which penetrates our hearts and thoughts with an inexpressible ecstasy.

At last the sun rests on the horizon, whichslowly swallows it. Our sad thoughts are drawn toward the West, towards France. For some of us that sun is gilding the faces of loved ones and caressing the windows of our homes; for others it is glimmering in the tearful eyes of a sweetheart. From our lips, like a messenger of feelings that cannot be written, its beams carry our kisses to lay on other lips.... But it also sweeps over fields bathed in the pure blood of our soldiers—and the thoughts of these "vagabonds" it bears onward toward their spoil.

Certain evenings, while the glorious sun is thus bearing away our dreams, the moon, languorous and discolored, rises laboriously over the Ionian Isles, and offers us her pale rays. But we do not look at her. For her sickly light, her capricious form, her pilgrimage among the shadows—all serve to remind us too painfully of the obscurity of our own labor, the uncertainty of our thoughts and the memory which our work will leave behind us to the ages.

Strait of Otranto, 18 October.

Day before yesterday the "naval army" gathered at the rendezvous appointed by the Admiral off Fano. It was a warm, clear day. The sea seemed asleep; light clouds came and went in the sky. From all directions gathered the squadrons, the divisions, and the separate vessels. Slow and thickset, the ironclads rose over thehorizon and moved down upon us. Round about them destroyers performed evolutions like greyhounds frolicking round a hunter. From Italy, from the Ionian Isles, raced black-striped cruisers, swift and graceful, plowing up the foam; they had left their monotonous patrol guard to join the French cohorts about to ascend the Adriatic.

At the rendezvous, crouching like a beautiful tiger in repose, and covered with flags and pennants, the *Courbet*, the Admiral's vessel, awaited the others. Breathless they paused beneath her gaze, and received their final orders. From the bridges of the *Courbet*, the signalmen, with movements of their arms, sent preliminary instructions to each ship; the many-colored signals ascended and descended the halyards. Boats and launches left the ships and hurried to the Admiral from whom the officers received long closed envelopes which they quickly carried back to their ships. The commanders opened them, bent over maps and plans, and divined the wishes of their chief.... Every week since we left Toulon this has been the episode which interrupts our tedious voyages. After it is over, our "naval army," numerous and impressive, again breaks up. One after another, the ships begin to churn the purple water, taking their proper posts and lines, and dispersing towards their regular night routes. The Admirals lead their squadrons and divisions; long dim streaks in the sky, far apart, indicate the tracks of our departure, but the fickle sea effaces all its lines. Towards the North, losing itself in the distance, the immense procession moves on to offer a tournament of battle. It stretches out the length of a province. Behind, and at a great distance from each other, the armored squadrons move at a slow and steady pace. At the head, offering their breasts, deploy the cruisers, sweeping the Adriatic. Ahead of them there is nothing but emptiness.

The *Waldeck-Rousseau* advances in the night. Tense with watching, she trembles in the darkness. All the ports, all the scuttles are closed, and not a particle of light betrays us. The fires are controlled, so that they throw off no sparks or cinders. Absolute silence prevails. Our invisible progress makes no more sound than the flight of a night-bird. It is my detachment which has the first watch.

There is a certain powerful excitement in concentrating all one's energy in ear and eye, in restraining the desire of the blood for sudden action. My comrade to port, I to starboard, do not stir. If our fingers mechanically touch our eyelids or scratch our itching neck, our intent eyes never waver. They see nothing but blackness. The light of the stars is veiled in a thin mist, and there are no reflections on the water. We move in a darkness as of the tomb. Thus, in the forest, animals creep along on guard, bending the weedsand crawling through the brush they do not even rustle. Our engines and screws drive us along, supple and furtive like groups of cats. Our prow cuts the water without stirring it.

Of this cautious being, my comrade and I are the temporary brain. Around us perhaps lurk Austrian destroyers, also invisible and silent, which may be launching at us, as they pass, their pointed torpedoes. Before we have suspected that death prowls there, they will have perceived a gigantic hulk making a spot in the darkness. Let the two officers on watch, safeguarding the ship, have a second of forgetfulness or fatigue, and a thousand men may be lost in the abyss whence none returns. In us these thousand sailors place implicit confidence. If disaster should happen, they would forgive us in their last agony, because they know that no human power could have prevented it. Presently, when we lie down on our bunks, worn out with the strain, we shall deliver our lives over to our successors without a thought. The two watchers on the bridge are the guardian angels of the crew.

That is the greatness of our vocation. Nowhere in this war, in which the battlefields will have seen so much heroism, will there be a heavier task imposed on leaders of men. No general or sergeant could commit a mistake which would annihilate his army or his squad in a single instant. The ball kills only one man, the shell carries offonly a file; and the mine spares those at a distance. Every fighter on land has his chance of surviving the worst disaster, and the most careless officer will never have upon his conscience the death of all the men he has commanded.

But a boat is a prison, more confining than stones and bars and chains; we are suspended over the abyss. Naval catastrophes are like a vomit from hell; no other catastrophe crushes so many lives at a single stroke. Lives and goods lost together! Terrible words, which cannot be said of cataclysms on land. Earthquakes, fires leave reminders, ruins, witnesses of that which was.... But the ocean tears from her surface a handful of metal and men, and sends them to rot in her bowels. And the next day the unchangeable deeps smile their eternal smile.

Long ago the sea knew the whole art of murder. Our diabolical genius had to add tenfold to the horror. Human ingenuity has invented the mine, more remorseless than a hundred reefs; the torpedo, more destructive than a hurricane, and those explosives which tear to pieces still living tissue into projectiles of flesh.

The slow night ebbs away. These forebodings of the fate of sailors invade the souls of the watchers, and make them long to vanquish the specters of the shadow. For to die is nothing if one has been able to save others. From the interior of the ship, from the hammocks and theposts of the watch, rises the voice of a hundred trusting hearts. That unity of appeal creates this thing which has neither form nor law, but which draws its strength from the very depths of the soul, in that affection, that complete devotion of oneself: Duty.

Tedious as are the hours filled with such distressing thoughts, the night, nevertheless, finally begins to fade. The East pales and the mists disappear and unveil the depths of the sky, where a few faint stars go out one after the other before the approach of the sun. The light slowly conquers the limits of space, and sea and ships take on form and substance. From the South a cruiser emerges, gray as the waves through which it comes, the dawn strips it of its veil, moulds its shape, reveals the masts and the smoke from its stacks. Farther away there is a row of motionless points on the surface of the water; these are the masts of the ironclads that have followed on our track. Others still farther South are entirely invisible.

The mountains of Austria and Montenegro take possession of a segment of the sky; their white peaks have a scarlet hem. They form a wall stretching from North to South, of which the ravines, the escarpments and the summits are still buried in mist. Our cruiser gets orders to bear farther northward, while the other cruisers deploybetween it and the ironclads. It puts on speed, its whole bulk quivering under its armor. When it has taken position, it can still see its neighbor in the South, and the stacks of the ship behind it. But only puffs of smoke reveal the presence of the other ships, of which the most distant is opposite Antivari or St. John of Medua, fifty kilometers away.

The entire "naval army" bears off to the right and moves toward the enemy coast, which every moment renders clearer. I take the watch, which has been resigned before midnight. A few hours of uneasy sleep have left me with the taste of ashes in my mouth, and a painful fluttering in my eyelids. But have we not all lived in this way for I know not how many weeks? And should one not whip up his blood in the face of approaching danger? And can one stay drowsy in the marvel of this dawn?

Here is light in all its purity and perfection. The blue of a young girl's eyes, or the delicate green of April meadows, seem gross and hard in comparison with this light. It is quiet, yet alive with beauty. It enchants like a perfume; it evokes a solemn rapture. Surely the robes of angels must be woven from rays of such light.

But from behind the mountains the sun rises. Objects appear more clearly and lose their delicacy of line. Far to the North over the Dalmatian Isles a few clouds stain the sky. The hazeis lifting from the bay of Cattaro, the details of which we study through our glasses—gray spots of forts, white streaks of lighthouses, smoke of Austrian ships sheltered in the roadstead. Above the town, which is still invisible, slowly rises a black point like a dark bubble; I watch this suspicious ascension, but cannot yet make out what it means. On the other side the sun hangs on the summit of a mountain.

All the air seems to vibrate. One's eyes are dazzled at such refulgence, such clearness. The sun frees himself from the mountain peaks, and as he rises pours down a triumphal torrent of light. The Dalmatian Isles, the Austrian coast rise suddenly, imposing and menacing. The cruisers to the South reflect a radiance from their hulls, the sheet of sea over which our cruiser advances alone is covered with a glassy surface which the eye cannot penetrate. With their hands on the mortar, the gunners stand stiller than ever. In the bow of the ship the sailors who do not belong to the watch keep their eyes on the approaching land and the gliding sea. The ascending black point has stopped, and seems held at the end of a line. Now I recognize it for a captive balloon. Its casing, its cording, looks as transparent as a spider's web. But from its height a human eye has observed us; the submarines and destroyers have been warned by telephone; and all is astir, in this inaccessible arsenal, with the effort to attack, without danger to themselves, the cruiser that offers them battle. In the splendor of the still morning, this captive balloon symbolizes the troubled passions of men—murder and destruction. But it is delightful to approach the enemy through all this enchantment. Under the sunlight the sea has become blue and seductive again, and the death of the cruiser, should it occur, will take on a sort of divine beauty in this brightness.

Things begin to happen. Out of the last bank of mist which stretches along the coast there mount in spiral flights two almost imperceptible insects. At so great a distance they resemble two animated bits of dust. They are Austrian aeroplanes seeking the height and the currents of air favorable for attack. They see the *Waldeck-Rousseau*, lost in the sea-mist, and instantly separate, one drawing northward, the other southward. In a few minutes their outlines are hidden in the clouds, and we no longer know what has become of them.

Soon the Montenegrin post of Lovcen signals us by wireless that the harbor of Cattaro is astir. A squadron of torpedo-destroyers is getting up steam. Some ironclads are moving, submarines are making for the channel outlet. Forewarned, the watchers on the bridge, sailors and officers, gaze at the narrows, and soon discern on the surface of the water some fine bluish tufts like the smoking butts of cigarettes. It takes the acute vision of seamen to distinguish them, for we are sailing more than twenty miles from shore. They are two submarines coming out of Cattaro and preparing to submerge. The brightness of the air is enough to dazzle us. And then we see nothing more. These metal fish are buried under the waves, taking unknown paths, and moving mysteriously towards us who are their prey.

All eyes on the bridge are fixed upon the scene. We approach danger with clear vision and mind and with a quiet pleasure. On the forward deck the marines not on duty scrutinize alternately the horizon and the faces of the officers on watch to make out what adventures they hold in store.... Among the winding straits of Cattaro glide masts as fine as hairs; these are the destroyers which in their turn are issuing forth to attack us. The *Waldeck-Rousseau* keeps on toward the hostile coast. At last the first destroyers appear, gray, and plumed with smoke; the moment has come to prepare ourselves for battle, and the commander orders the trumpets sounded to clear the decks for action.

At the first notes of this music which they have heard so many times for mere drill, the sailors prick up their ears and cast questioning glances at the bridge. Voices are raised asking nervously: "Is it in earnest this time?" With an affirmative nod I reassure them. A joyous clamor rises from all their hearts, the clamor of children who are at last going to play. In an instant everyone has rushed to his post of battle. The decks are deserted, the ship is abandoned.

But in its bosom a hidden life goes forward. The port stanchions are closed; the powerful bolts, which the men hastily shoot, make out of the enormous hull a hive partitioned by steel. In every cell of the hive groups of men, sometimes a single man, look after the apparatus, set it working, and wait. They see nothing, and will see nothing. If the ship is conquered, they will not know how or why. Everyone is silent. Where soldiers in the great moment of battle translate their joy of action into shouting, sailors, on the contrary, must keep absolute silence. Only the rattle of the engines, the telephone orders, and the trumpet calls may be heard. In the turrets and the casemates, behind the guns, the gunners and pointers hold themselves motionless, ready for the swift, precise movements, repeated so many times in innumerable drills, which will send straight to their mark the rain of well-aimed shells.

From the guns, the engines, the helm, the mute tension of a thousand men flows back to the turret, the brain of a cruiser. In this armored enclosure are stationed the commander, his two officers in charge of the firing, his navigating officer. They know that the safety of the ship depends on the clearness of their judgment. With lowered voices, as if they were conversing on matters of no importance, they address sailors who transmit their orders. Crouching before the artillery keyboard, a few men manipulate the fly-wheels, the bells and signals which tell the orchestra of guns their distances, correct their aim, give them orders to fire. Behind the three dials which direct the engines three sailors quickly write the orders. To right and left, mouth and ear to a line of telephones and speaking trumpets, two sailors listen to the word from below and reply. With his hand on the lever of the steering-gear, and his eyes on the compass of the route, an impassive petty-officer executes the orders of maneuver. There is no noise except the slight grating of the rudder indicating each degree to starboard or port. Through the horizontal embrasures of the turret, like the narrow iron-barred slits in the helmets of knights, the four officers survey the horizon. They make out the churning of foam from a periscope which is moving toward the cruiser's starboard at top speed. Instantly the whole volley of light guns opens fire on this enemy; the rudder is turned to starboard to change the course of the cruiser, deceive the submarine, and attempt to ram it.... Almost at the same moment there appears from the clouds to the northward an aeroplane, which descends towards us like a water-spout, and wheels about, trying to get a long-distance aim. Our sharpshooters cover this enemy of the air, and their shots crackle above us like drums. As soon as we are close enough to fight the charging destroyers effectively, our heavy guns open a steady fire on them. Our cruiser becomes a mass of smoke and noise as it confronts the triple peril of air, surface and deep. Every man works with the precision of a clock. I cannot begin to enumerate all the episodes of these exciting moments....

Three hundred meters above us, the aviator lets loose his bombs. Their fall makes a noise like the rending of a sheet of iron. But the turn of the cruiser to starboard has defeated the precision of his aim. Near our hull, fore and aft, they burst with an uproar which deadens the voice of the guns; bits of them rebound to the decks and turrets, and around the spot where they have exploded the sea quivers as if it had been peppered with a hail of pebbles. The aviator mounts higher, pursued by our sharpshooters, who, however, soon abandon him.

Despite the turn to starboard, the cruiser misses the submarine by a few feet, and it disappears beneath the water. The sailors below hear a rippling and lapping of water pass along the hull; they even think they feel the impact of a solid object which scrapes the keel without being able to penetrate it. There is very little doubt but that the submarine did torpedo us, but the quick maneuver of the ship saved us. Instead of hitting us squarely, and damaging our sides, the torpedo—perhaps there were several—merely grazed us and passed on without effect.

In order to see whether it has touched us and to get another aim at us, the submarine comes to the surface again; as it rises we see its periscope and turret athwart us, and without delay the light guns cover it a second time. The water boils about it, the shells burst and envelop it in yellowish smoke. Had it been struck? Is it destroyed? One never knows the fate of these enemies, which, whether victor or vanquished, immediately submerge. The course of the cruiser sweeps us far ahead; we no longer concern ourselves with the submarine, which is no menace to us now. Only our heavy guns speak.

At a great distance the Austrian torpedo-destroyers are encircled by our falling shells. But, like the snipes they are, they twist and zig-zag on the water. We rush along at a speed of eleven meters a second; and if our fire halts the destroyers, it does not seem to touch them. Their prudence triumphs over their boldness. Persuaded that our fire will never admit them within torpedoing distance, they describe a half-circle and flee. In succession, like rabbits regaining their burrow, they take shelter in the channel of Cattaro, until we distinguish only the tips of their masts, which recede, and disappear.

Our heavy guns next engage the coast-works, lighthouses, or batteries, which are now in range. Since the explosions on rocks and earth enable us to regulate our fire, we should shortly be doing great damage to the shore, except for a wireless from the commander-in-chief ordering us to cease our solitary combat. Doubtless the land forts are waiting for us to come nearer, and their guns, more powerful than ours, will do us more harm than the aviator, the submarine and the destroyers together.

Regretful but obedient, the *Waldeck-Rousseau* turns her back on the shore and moves southward toward the waiting cruisers. In a few seconds their distant outlines, as well as the squadrons of ironclads, grow large and stand out in relief against the sky. They would all have come to our rescue if our challenge had succeeded in drawing out the powerful armament sheltered in Cattaro. But once more the Austrians fail to offer battle, having attempted only to send the *Waldeck-Rousseau* to her death, with the smallest possible loss to themselves.

While our cruiser regains her own division at top speed, the periscope of a second submarine, on watch in the offing, reveals its furrow of foam on our port side. Regardless of whether it has launched its torpedoes, we rain upon it a steady fire from our lighter guns, not pausing to pursue it, for the order to return is imperative. Halfan hour later the *Waldeck-Rousseau* slows down and again takes her place in the line of cruisers. Their crews look with envy upon this vessel, the first in the naval war to have the triple honor of facing the triple enemies of the ships.

Two signals are raised. We take new positions for descending the Adriatic. In a few days we shall come back to insult Austria, and perhaps we shall be more fortunate. It is now the end of a white, translucent morning. On board, the battle organization is abandoned, the ordinary watch resumed. While the officers and sailors on the bridges continue to study the sea, we meet again in the ward-room. Meal-time approaches, no one mentions the moments through which the cruiser has just lived. A certain officer of engineers comes out of the boiler-room and tries to beat his record at cup and ball, playing with a steady hand. Four others, their ears still filled with the roar of the guns, plunge into the peaceful subtleties of "bridge." Others examine maps of Flanders and Poland.

In a profound calm, a kind of oblivion, we talk of things remote from war. And when, after the meal, the commander assembles the officers in the saloon to celebrate in a glass of champagne their baptism of fire, his speech already seems to call up an event from the far past.

Adriatic Sea, 25 October.

Something dark brushes the horizon. A spot on the sky? A storm cloud? The mirage of an island? Our eyes do not hesitate for long; the thing lives and breathes; it is the smoke of a vessel. The officer on watch speeds up the engines, changes the rudder, and points the bow toward this smoke. Since our departure from France not a ship, not a sail, has evaded investigation by our cruisers and destroyers, the Argus and Cerberus of the ocean paths.

Above the horizon rise the masts, the stacks, the hull of the ship. Innocent or guilty, it knows it cannot escape our speed, and does not attempt to flee. At fifteen thousand meters, its outline indicates whether it is a liner, or a freighter; at ten thousand, its displacement shows us whether it is loaded or carries no cargo; at five thousand, its flag reveals its nationality. If it be English or French, it is allowed to pass. If neutral, we show it the signal of the international code: "Halt immediately!"

It has to stop. If it shows any inclination to pursue its way, the first blank shot warns it not to play with fire. If it pretends not to hear this reprimand, a shell falls in its path to inform it that we are not joking. If it insists upon proceeding, a few shots straight at its hull assure it that the matter is becoming serious. It always stops in time.

The cruiser halts within range of the suspect. In an instant one of our long-boats has been lowered and its crew seizes the oars. An officer, armed with sword and revolver and carrying a big record-book, jumps into the boat, which puts off from our vessel. A sailor accompanies him. When the wind is rough and the sea choppy, the boat bounds, plunges and rolls on this passage which seems interminable; the seven sailors struggle with all their might at the oars; buckets of water drench the heads of officer and men; in a few minutes they are soaked through.

The long-boat accosts the steamer, from the rail of which hangs a rope ladder, sometimes merely a knotted rope. Why are they always too short? I don't know. Anyway the officer, hampered by his sword and his register, and strangled in a uniform which was never meant for jumping, stretches out his arms and tries to grasp the ladder. But the swell rolls back and forth and tips the boat. As he approaches the ship, there is the ladder swaying two meters above him; as soon as he is high enough to seize it, the ship lurches off. It is like a skittish horse that refuses the mount. At these gymnastics the passengers and crew of the ship smile maliciously. The officer rages. He puts his sword between his teeth, his register between coat and shirt, waits for the least unfavorable moment, launches himself headlong—and grasps the ladder. For a few seconds he performs on this flying trapeze. A playful wave laps his knees, his hips, his chest. Recovering himself, he makes a few rungs, hoists himself up the slippery ropes, throws his leg over the rail, and at last puts his foot on the deck.

This adventure, thank heaven, is not always so unpleasant! Some visits seem like pleasant duties. But what has the bad winter weather in store for us?

It would be demanding superhuman virtue from the captains to expect them to like these visits on the high seas. We delay them, we bore them, and sometimes we turn them away from their route. Ordinarily they show us a very surly face; too polite a mien, on the other hand, is to be distrusted. The officer readjusts his disordered uniform, controls his ill-humor, assumes an impassive air, and gives a military salute.

"Captain," he says, "have the kindness to show me your papers."

This formula is pronounced in English, Spanish, Italian or French. Grammar sometimes suffers, but not all the world is polyglot. When the visiting officer has exhausted all his vocabularies without anyone's understanding him, he contents himself with a gesture, reinforced by a contraction of his brows in the direction of his revolver. Thereupon intelligence comes to the most obtuse. A little procession forms. The captain looking important, the officer severe, the commissary obsequious, the sailor escort bringing up the rear; by means of the passage and stairs these four actors in the little drama reach the navigation room, where are kept the regulation papers. The more luxurious liners sometimes set a table with cigars and liqueurs in the first cabin. Such an attention arouses double suspicion.

The passengers line up along the deck. This episode makes a pleasant interruption in the monotony of the voyage, and gives their pacific minds a slight shuddering taste of the great war. Every man begins to feel like a hero, and to invent a tale which will astonish his future hearers. The men search the face of the French officer, but read little on this cold mask. The women, bolder, solicit his glances, his smile, press themselves on his attention. "Vive la France!" cries one. "He has a real revolver!" whispers another, shuddering. "Stop, officer, and let me photograph you!" begs a third.

The visiting officer does not reply, does not stop, but hastens on his mission. In his register he consults the original of all the documents he has warrant to verify; text, stamps, signatures are exactly reproduced, and not one word of the ship's papers must differ from the original. If they are in Arabic, Norwegian or Japanese, the officer's pencil compares them line by line. In curt phrases he approves or objects.

The civil status of the ship seems correct; its name, its country, its record, reveal nothing ambiguous. The captain is then questioned. Whence has he come, where is he going, and where has he stopped? What are the owners' orders? The chart and the log, the dates and hours of calls at ports, certified by the official authorities, are all verified. The slightest inaccuracy requires explanations, proofs. In such times as these, all movements at sea must be above suspicion, and the least evasion renders one suspect. To help his captain the ship's commissary bustles about, pours a glass of liqueur, uncorks a bottle of champagne, introduces a foaming glass between two incisive questions. But the French officer courteously waves aside these seductions.

The commissary in his turn goes on the stand; he spreads out and explains the bills of merchandise, illegible scrawls in every language, dotted with strange abbreviations, with obsolete weights and measures in the jargon of grocer and manufacturer. Every line has them, and twenty special dictionaries could not disclose their traps. Like an archæologist poring over a worn stone, the visiting officer weighs, unravels, interprets these hieroglyphics; from a pocket-book he extracts lists of shippers and consignees friendly to our enemies, and inspects the ship's papers to see that their names do not figure on them.

Every bill of merchandise raises a question. Certain cargoes always go through, others under certain conditions, some, officially contraband, are fair booty. The texts of the treaties of The Hague and of London pretend to solve all these problems. The officer consults these texts, looking for helpful suggestions. But these treaties, drawn up in times of peace for the despair of sailors in war, are full of ambiguities, over which the crafty neutrals slide. How many enigmas does not the officer have to solve in a few minutes under the dull gaze of his two colleagues!

According to such and such a paragraph the case appears clear, but a footnote throws everything into confusion again. There are neither precedents nor regulations. Upon our decision rests a fraction of our country's honor. Too much good nature runs us the risk of providing our enemies with valuable materials; too much rigor will bring vigorous complaints from injured neutrals. Let our decision leave a loophole in the dispute, and learned jurists will deliberate over it in the prize-courts for weeks and months; then will consume endless hours and heaps of paper before discovering what ought to be the judgment actually rendered in the interval between a drenching in a long-boat and a submarine scare.

Bah! We have our privileges of State. Our conscience is clear, our intentions are pure, and little remorse accompanies our verdicts. Yesterday, as well as to-morrow, we make a seizure or release, according to the simple dictates of common sense. The smiles and grimaces of the commissary do not warp our judgments; even when the captain, at a critical moment, presses on us a whole box of choice Havana cigars this seduction adds not a grain to our weighing-scale. The officer politely declines, ends his examination, makes his decision, and demands the passenger list.

"Captain, have the kindness to draw up on deck all the persons on board. Let each one hold his identification papers in his hand. In five minutes I shall make my inspection."

Women, stewards and waiters scatter through the cabins, which suddenly fill with commotion. In the midst of a chorus of exclamations, of murmurs and laughs, feverish fingers ransack writing cases and bags; travelers with good consciences easily discover what they need; the women adjust their hair, hastily powder a suspicion of tan on their faces, and with a turn of their hand put all the details of their toilette in order. They are tremendously entertained. It's like a real play! For a very little more they would put on their prettiest gowns.... But the officer is in a hurry, and the captain excuses himself: one passenger cannot lay his hand on his passports, which he has certainly shut up in a trunk. Exactly! The story is well-known! That bird from Germany must be held.

Everyone lines up in two or more rows. Irresistibly, an order rises to the lips of the visiting officer—"Right dress! Eyes front!" But no, these passengers are not soldiers. And now the task is to keep in line this fat lady in a rather short skirt, who inserts herself between an asthmatic youth and a rugged American. Let us stifle our laughter! The lines sway, somewhere at the back a boy sneezes, two Brazilians or Argentinians burst into shameless laughter, a huge negro trembles with fear. The officer passes on his inspection.

Like a row of blind people holding out their wooden bowls, everyone carries his passport in his hand. The men are extremely grave, almost indignant, and one can imagine the silent perturbation behind their brows. They lie in wait for an imprudent word in order that they may at once invoke their counsel, their ambassador, and the unwritten laws of neutrals. Vain hope! The officer looks them over swiftly, and opens their papers with a scrupulous touch. Stamps and signatures are correct, the descriptions too; the passports, the certificate of nationality, have no taint of fraud. But no touchstone is worth so much as that of speech: to expert ears a few words, a few phrases, reveal many secrets, and a hesitating manner accuses where the documents acquit.

"Kindly tell me where you come from....Kindly tell me your name and the date of your birth.... Did you leave your country some time ago? Kindly answer me in your own language.... What is your profession?"

One has to question closely and in various ways, and keep oneself from getting into dialogues. There is never a discussion; an immediate judgment, and we go on.

Compatriots, Russians, English, undergo the questioning. They are cheerful and anxious to chat.

"In too much of a hurry, my friend!... A handshake and bon voyage!... The last news from the wireless?... Everything goes well, very well!"

Click! Click! Right and left, the kodaks are at work. Who will ever count the albums in which playful passengers have put their naval inspection? They imagine they have not been seen, but their faces, suddenly serious, and their air of having touched nothing, betray their crime.

"And you, mademoiselle? What signatures on your passport? What journey are you making?"

"I am from Valparaiso, and I am on my way to my family in Moscow!"

Ye gods! What are all these women doing wandering about the vast world? Half the soldiers in Europe have thrown themselves on the other half, but travelers come and go like doves, without thought of trouble.

The passports of the men are comprehensible—functionaries, manufacturers going from port to port, mobilized men, producers from the Far East; all avow intentions which are definite and easy to deal with. But the origin and destination of the women are puzzling enigmas. In America, in Asia, in Africa, all the chancelleries of remote consulates have written over and scratched out the most bewildering itineraries. These papers are fantastic.

The mystery is increased by the contradictions of the passengers' appearance. The visiting officer examines a modest passenger in tennis shoes, flannel suit and traveling cap, who blushes like a boarding-school miss, and answers very timidly. And what does he see on the photograph of the passport she shows him? A smiling doll, buried under a hat as large as a millstone, adorned with aigrettes and feathers; a very elaborate arrangement of the hair which hides half her face, and three rows of pearls on her bare throat. Is there anything in common between this luxurious figure and the timid person wringing her hands in the line, whose inward mirth appears in her sparkling eyes and an imperceptible trembling of her elbows? He would be a perjurer who would swear to it.

It is even a relief when they know their own nationality exactly. I never suspected that one's native country could be mislaid, lost and found like a pair of gloves. But in these latitudes one learns something every day. Wars, treaties, and revolts, have so confused the map of the East that it seems as if every passenger were provided with two or three spare countries.

"Now, Madam, will you explain for your husband, whom I do not understand? What is his nationality? And you yourself, are you Turkish, Egyptian, Greek or Russian?"

"It is very simple, Mr. Officer. My husband was Armenian, that is to say, a Turkish subject. At the time of the massacres he fled to the Caucasus and found it wise to put himself under Russian protection. His business called him to Crete, which became Greek while he was living there. I was born in Macedonia, a Turkish subject, but the last war has made me a Serb. We went to Alexandria because it was quieter there, for since the English are suzerains of Egypt, we intended...."

So goes the story. Adventuresses, spies, or wanderers tossed about in Levantine eddies, their talk is as picturesque as their papers. It would be absurd to persecute them in this maze where they are astray.

To what end, moreover? The real prize, the choice booty, is recognized by infallible signs: German faces, Teutonic accents, insolent or honeyed replies, stammered explanations. However much they may have garbled their names andsubmitted to us false ones in writing, the race of these Germans oozes from every pore. They are on their way to foment rebellion in Egypt or in Tripoli; they are going to work the Balkans, to pursue in India or China their secret intrigues. Invariably their passports derive from Switzerland or Holland, but their certificates of nationality, very new, just off the press, remind one of coins that are counterfeit and too bright. Suspects!... The officer goes down to their cabins; everything he finds in the valises, the steamer trunks, denotes innocence and sincerity. But he is nauseated by a strange odor. It cannot be defined, but whoever has smelt it recognizes unerringly the kind of flesh it comes from. With handkerchief to nose; he turns over the bed and ransacks the furniture. Under the mattress, behind the wash-basin, in the folds of a blanket, lies the fatal paper, the envelope or the packet.... Enemies!...

Now the affair must be ended decisively, elegantly, in the French style. Invested with discretionary powers on a neutral boat, the visiting officer conforms to courtesies which would satisfy the most exacting. His attitude, the tone of his voice, his words, affirm, in surroundings often hostile, always excited, the sovereign will of his country. The staff-officer of the boat, the crew and the passengers form a hostile jury of free witnesses who would jeer to the ends of the earththe slightest clumsiness. But we are at any rate vain enough not to imitate the ruffianly manners of our enemies.

The visiting officer stops before the German, calls him by name, lays a finger lightly on his sleeve or shoulder, and says, without raising his voice:

"I take you prisoner. Follow my sailor, who will carry your baggage and conduct you to the ship's boat."

Cries, bursts of rage, insults, are of no avail. One adds nothing. What is said is said. At the worst, if the scene becomes painful, the officer turns to the captain.

"Commandant, I direct you to use your authority to compel Monsieur to follow me. Otherwise I shall be obliged to use force. I take the responsibility for the order I give you, and I will draw up for you a report of the proceedings."

That is enough. Protected by the owners and his government, the captain abandons the prisoner to his fate, and speeds the removal of his baggage. The German taken in the snare protests, sheepish and mortified. But the faithful sailor has already seized him and is hurrying him without much ado to the long-boat. The audience makes comments. The kodaks work their fastest. A few hands applaud, a few malcontents murmur. The circle opens deferentially before the officer, who copies on the log the formulas appropriateto the visit, recounts the incident, exonerates the captain, and signs the deposition which will go the round of the chancelleries.

Then, and only then, when the business is all settled, will he accept perhaps a cigarette, or a file of newspapers, or a cup of coffee. While the prisoner's baggage is being somehow tumbled into the bottom of the long-boat, the officer takes a few steps along the deck. The crowd of passengers precipitate themselves upon his suddenly humanized person. "News! News!" implore all the voices. He repeats the wireless messages received from the Eiffel Tower, from Poldhu, and is careful to make no comments. As if by magic, the misses, the donnas and senoras of all the nations and of every type of beauty slide under his hand a pencil, albums, post-cards. He defends himself. They beg with alluring glances. Must he not yield? Feverishly he scrawls, signs, dates the cards and albums. He is promised photographs—which he never receives. Sly scissors clip from his coat a button to mount on a hatpin. Families invite him to the Ukraine, to California, to Buenos Aires, after the war is over.

Finally the sailor escort returns: "Ready!" he says, saluting.

The officer pushes his way through the crowd, throws his leg over the rail, commences his tumbling descent. On the seat of the boat the prisoner, quite still, takes up the least possible room.

"You may continue your voyage!" cries the visitor to the captain, who is awaiting his release.

More questions, and farewells; a waving of scarfs and handkerchiefs. But he is already in the hollow of the waves; he wipes the spray from his face, and, raising his cap, makes a fine salute of farewell to all these passengers whom he will never see again.

Ten minutes later the boat with its prisoner is hoisted on board. The officer reports to his commandant, and at once draws up his statement. The cruiser begins to move, heading west; the liner recedes to the south, and soon we see nothing but her smoke. For several hours we prowl about, expecting the same ceremony to recommence. Five or six times a day we stop, make a visit, permit them to go on, or show our teeth. There are some amusing and some dramatic adventures, but for a few profitable visits how many futile ones there are! Yesterday in battle; always on the watch; a beast hunting for prey; the customs-officer of the high sea; traveling ceaselessly; never in port—such is the lot of the cruiser. Who of us reckoned on this as war? No one, I swear.

North of Corfu, 30 October.

Was it not a dream from which we have just emerged? For several days—no, I must be mistaken—for a few hours the *Waldeck-Rousseau* has been lying in the harbor of Malta, and our feet have trod the ground, the shore, the sidewalks. Fifty-three days at sea had persuaded us that everything in the world is in motion. One has to be a sailor to appreciate the delights of the shore.

It was in fact a dream. To-night finds us again on our patrol, between the coasts of Epirus and Corfu. Our rest is brief, we move very slowly, the screws seem almost asleep, and during my watch, from ten in the evening until two in the morning, the cruiser has slipped through magnificent shadows.

This sea is too lovely. Anxious to solace our exile with her feminine caresses, she shows us from hour to hour a delicious and ever-changing countenance. In moments of alarm and trial she succeeds in pervading us with her gentle consolation. But to-day, far from the Austrian coast, everything seems kindly, and the sailor can abandon himself to the magic of the shadows. Not a sound, not a breath, in these happy moments. Nature never slumbers so softly as on the sleeping waves, and the most smothered words are too noisy to express this silence. The sea opens languorously at our prow, and receives us amorously, so to speak, in her watery arms, which embrace us tenderly along our hull. The reflections of the stars, which ordinarily rock without ceasing up and down the ridges of water, stand motionless in it like nails of light. The coast is mirrored in the black element, reversed so perfectly that the land and its image seem cut from the same block. Epirus, Corfu and Merlera surround us in an immense circle, enclosing us almost as in a lake. But this lake is filled with a limpid water that extends from the shores of yesterday to the cliffs of to-morrow.

Enlarged in the transparent air, the stars seem to have come down nearer to us; the moon does not disturb the happy shadow. The star Sirius rises in the heavens, detached suddenly from the mountains like a slow rocket. She is round like some heavenly fruit, and the beacons on the coast are dim before this queen of our heaven.

On the Balkan cliff, halfway up the side of the mountain, flames a red light. Evidently it is a conflagration; in some little valley a wretched village is burning and expiring. Is it Albanian, Greek or Epirote? Some bandits with torches have set on fire the first barn on their path; the thatch, the mud walls, the dim huts, are consumed in whirlwinds, and the starlight is stained with streaks of smoke. The herds up there bleat and bellow in the flames; disheveled mothers carry off their nurslings; the men load their guns and unloose the dogs. To-morrow, in reprisal, another hamlet will be burned.

We are so far away, so lost in the night, that this sinister fire does not affect us at all. Why pity or curse, when distance smothers all sound? Yet how can we help being carried back to the obsession of the war, which the sea, the sky, and the stars, had banished from the present moment? Have not these distant flames been lighted by the incendiary of Berlin, and do they not portend the track of murder that will soon soak the East in blood?

But on this night I do not wish to abandon myself to sorrow. I wish to let my whole being slip into the rich blackness, and to ask of it the serenity demanded for the coming danger. Before dawn a velvety freshness creeps up, and banishes my insidious fatigue. This freshness of the end of night seems to make still smoother the surface of the sea, in which are sunk the reflections of the stars, clear, numberless, white as wax. Sparkling above each taper, every star recalls the flame which trembles on Christian altars at dusk, when the tardy penitent cannot distinguish the dim wick between the wax and the fire. Among the unreal columns of this Adriatic temple glides the cruiser.

This temple has neither nave, organ, nor pavement. The chandeliers have burned there since the first breath of things. The tabernacle is the immensity wherein swing the divine planets. The nameless architect is God, who has sown the stars near His throne in order that the humble regard of men shall be lifted to Him.

Among the Austrian Islands, 2 November.

It is dawn. We are moving in a long file towards the Austrian islands. From cruiser to cruiser the cocks are calling and answering each other. As their clear call salutes the dawn, it is accompanied by the cackling of our poultry-yard. In the fresh air the melancholy cattle are lowing, and the restless sheep are bleating; each of our dinners diminishes their number. To the officers on watch there rises the country smell from the henhouses, the cattle manure, and the hay, their fodder; and the air is filled with all the sounds of an awakening farm. Into the preoccupations of the watch creep precious memories and nostalgia; one would like to be in some country place, surrounded by meadows and woods, and one wants to close one's eyes so that nothing may destroy the dream.

But it is the green sea that forms our meadows; and the Dalmatian Isles, which emerge from the mist, are the groves of our horizon. The three big cruisers with six stacks are in the upper Adriatic, at the approaches to Lissa, a bastion of the Austrians on that sea, over which we sail without opposition. Further south, toward the isles of Lagosta or Pelagosa, the armored squadrons move at reduced speed. Once again, the tenth or twentieth time—we have lost count—the French "naval army" emerges from the dawn and offers the challenge they will not accept.

Only a short distance away, Lissa wakens under our eyes. Pleasant wooded slopes clothe this island; a tiny town, the principal place, surrounds a quiet harbor. We do not need our glasses to count the houses or even the windows; the people who come into the streets raise their hands to Heaven at sight of us and retreat behind their doors, which they barricade. The ribbon of water separating us from the shore is hardly broader than a river, and without taking aim our guns could pulverize houses and people. The Germans, in our place, would assure themselves a tremendous triumph, which their journals would celebrate in the list of German victories. But the French are incorrigible; they will never learn these illustrious methods, and will never destroy defenseless cities and men. Think what you will, our gospel contains no such precept.

Our division is accompanied by two squadrons of destroyers; they make their presence known by doing legitimate damage. The lighthouse of Lissa might assist the movement of Austrian ships at night; the cable can transmit to the arsenals news of the movements of the French fleet. Our destroyers do not hesitate to destroy these tools of war. Their guns thunder against the lighthouse; their dredges search for the cable at the bottom of the sea. To emphasize the ease with which we approach the enemy, small French vessels enter the harbor of Lissa with a haughty air. The fisherfolk and other people on the coast are terrified; no one expects mercy; everyone commends his soul to God. From the bridge the officers of the cruiser observe all this excitement; they see swarms of people fleeing into the country, where our guns could nail them like flies against the wall. It all makes us smile. Our sailors are quietly washing their linen, or gaily chattering. Like their officers, they are savoring the deliciousness of this quiet morning, in front of this island filled with sunlight and with terror. Their generous souls do not desire the destruction of this defenseless town. But at the bottom of their hearts and their talk lies a question which three months of naval warfare had not solved—"What must be done to these Austrians to make them revenge themselves? Will they make us no return for our insults?"

An officer and some sailors from the destroyers set foot on land. The population is humble and suppliant. We ask them the names and addresses of the two principal notables of the island, and immediately the notables are made known to us. No threats or revolvers! Everything goes off admirably. The two notables are brought before the chief of the French detachment; they tremble at first, but the courteous firmness of the all-powerful sailor reassures and conquers them. When it is announced to them that the Navy will hold them as hostages, they are not afraid to deliver themselves over to the good faith of men who do not abuse the rules of war. When we demand from Lissa a contribution of twenty-five thousand francs, they give it themselves, in hard cash of full weight, convinced that this gold is not passing into the pockets of highwaymen. When they are asked to deliver themselves up on board the torpedo-destroyers, they are given time to dress in their best clothes, to embrace their wives and children, and to assure the city that the enemy cruisers will not bombard it. In this little corner of the world where fate confers upon us these extraordinary powers, a few hours are sufficient to make the people our friends. If by any chance French victory should mean that the tricolor is planted on this island, it will float on friendly soil there.

Morning passes. Halted before the harbor of Lissa, the three cruisers wait while the destroyers finish their task at leisure. Midday sounds. Beyond doubt, the Austrian bases of Cattaro, Pola, and Sebenico have been notified of our action. The early hours of the afternoon pass. No enemy squadron appears to take up the challenge. Will our armed forces below the horizon have to wait in vain for the wireless announcing that our enemy will avenge the insult offered their territory? Is France really at war with Austria? The commander of the squadrons comes to make his report to the rear-admiral of the *Waldeck-Rousseau*. He tells of the terror of the inhabitants of Lissa, their meekness, the taking of two hostages on board his destroyer. Our wireless requests supplementary orders from the Commander-in-Chief. Suddenly, emerging from the maze of the Austrian islands, appear at last two columns of smoke. All the glasses and telescopes are turned towards these longed-for shadows. Our hearts leap; our eyes fear they are mistaken. But no! The enemy is replying to the insult. Numerous masts are graven on the horizon. Everyone sees them rise, and whenever a new one appears utters a cry of joy. Five! Ten! Fifteen! Eighteen! The great Day has come.

The sun shines brightly. Not a ripple breaks the sea. Our rear-admiral hoists signals of chase and combat, the division of cruisers and two squadrons of destroyers advance with all speed toward the hostile smoke. As yet we do not know the strength, the number, the armament, of this enemy who offers battle. What matter! The tops of its stacks cover the northwest sky. We must hasten to the fray. If our first engagement is not victorious, the wireless calls we send to the battleships will bring them hurriedly to the victory we have led up to with our first attack. Joyous trumpets sound to clear the decks for action; the ships of France hoist the shield of battle, the national flag, perfectly new, at the junction of two masts. In a few minutes all the men arerunning to their posts. They laugh, they sing, they are crazy with excitement. But hardly have they reached their apparatus than they have regained the silence of duty. Firemen at the fires, engineers at the engines, gunners at the guns, have prompt arms, steady spirits, and alert eyes. Along the hull the spray leaps and glides, like the road beside an automobile. In the turret the commandant, the firing officers, and the maneuver officer, await anxiously the moment when they will recognize the enemy as he presents himself to us. They want to increase the speed of the ship, but our screws are already turning madly; they cannot add a millimeter to our speed. At last, on the curve of the sea, are clearly drawn the outlines of our enemy.

Alas! They are nothing but destroyers! Rapid and powerful destroyers, indeed; but Austria could have afforded to offer us antagonists equal to ourselves. Let us be content with the windfall. Too many days have been squandered against invisible enemies. These are real, living, and full of fight. They gallop towards us, with torpedoes leveled. We point our guns, which cannot yet reach them. The match is even. Like us, they have hoisted the flag of battle; and the *Waldeck-Rousseau*, springing over the water like a full-blooded steed, leads the cruisers and the two squadrons to the adventure where death awaits.

A few minutes of anxious silence pass. Shutin the cells below, the men listen, trying to catch the heavy sound of the first broadside; they would be killed in an instant if a well-aimed torpedo should touch the cruiser, but they devote their stalwart souls to the machinery and the engines, that no one may be wanting in this crisis. Through their telescopes the gun-pointers watch the distance vanishing as if by miracle. Twenty thousand meters.... Eighteen thousand.... Fifteen thousand.... Fourteen thousand.... Only two thousand more, and the rattle of our artillery will rain upon the enemy. In three parallel lines the Austrian destroyers throw out torrents of smoke, which seem to merge; each line glides over the blue water like a shining serpent. Around us our own destroyers have closed up, and are plowing up clods of spray silvered by the sunlight.

But what is this! The Austrian lines swerve, deflect; their head makes a great curve! Is it possible? They would retreat! They would refuse an engagement! We are so angry that our eyes refuse to believe the retreat. It is an illusion of the light; a jest of the wind that makes the smoke bend. Not at all. They complete the circle, turn their backs on us, and fly off at top speed like three trains along their rails of foam.

Oh! To have this revenge in sight for so many futile weeks, and then to see it escape just at the point where our guns cannot reach! To feelthat the great engines under our feet, strong as they are, are unable to catch the prey, because its legs are too long! To measure the distance, and feel it increase a little with every second, like an elastic band of air stretched between us! Fourteen thousand meters!

Fourteen thousand one hundred.... Fourteen thousand two hundred. Ah! we should like to be able to control the waves, to throw into the air a sudden squall, to chop up a sea of billows and swells. Our own powerful keels would not be slowed down, but the destroyers would run foul of each crest of the waves, would slacken, become exhausted, and our mettle would triumph over their cowardice.

They make speed towards the labyrinth of the Dalmatian Isles, which loom before us as a family of marine monsters might emerge from the water. We continue the pursuit. Sixteen thousand meters.... Seventeen thousand meters.... Perhaps remorse or faintness will seize the cowards. But no, their confusion is a premeditated ruse. Up in the sky, gliding and descending through the transparent clouds, an aviator drops toward the French ships, enfilades them, and lets fall on us bombs which only the cleverest tacking evades; they burst against the hulls. One of the cruisers catches the wake of a periscope on the surface of the water. It may be that some prowling submarine has already fired its torpedoes,and our speed has deluded it; no one is affected. We shell the path of this streak of foam, which immediately vanishes. The submarine flees below the water, the aeroplane is already out of sight, the destroyers are nearing the entrance to the islands. Eighteen thousand meters.... Nineteen thousand.... Each second of pursuit increases the danger, the useless danger which has no chance of reward. It is becoming evident that this Parthian flight leads us into the zone where other submarines are prowling, and other aviators lurking, where slumber dangerous mines, which can inflict slaughter without stirring from their position. Why excite ourselves? We are rushing towards a death that will bring no glory to the Navy, no benefit to France. Austria will have a victory which will not even have *achetée son courage*.

The rear-admiral has the signals hoisted. While the Austrian destroyers are hidden in the straits into which they hope to draw us, our cruisers and destroyers make a wide detour in the offing; our engines carry us disdainfully away from these coasts which shelter no gallant enemy. One by one, from the depths of the ship, the men who have been enclosed during the combat come out again. They have seen and heard nothing, and they eagerly ask the news. The sailors on deck talk to them in a low voice. Their cheeks turn pale, they clench their hands, their eyes flash withrage. The dejected crew moves silently up and down. Their faces are melancholy, their hearts sore, their nerves seem to have lost their spring.

At twilight, a few hours later, we call together the "naval army." By means of the wireless messages sent during our chase, the ships have followed with passionate interest the enthusiasm, effort, dangers, and disappointments we have been through. Ready enough to help us, and to give the Austrian fleet a good reception had it come out, they are awaiting us for still another descent of the Adriatic, also to be unfruitful, like so many others. For half an hour, under the golden beams of the setting sun, the squadrons go through the usual maneuvers and get their sailing orders for the night. The majestic, supple lines cross one another, approach and recede upon the parade ground of the sea. Every movement is perfect; the scene resembles a procession of moving cathedrals. In the evening light the hulls take on all the colors of stained windows. The water is strewn with azure and purple flowers. The signals run up and down the masts. Into the sky rise curls of smoke. A religious silence prevails.

The night falls. Up among the islands, enveloped in mist, the Austrians can observe our contemptuous evolutions and our dignified departure. Not one of our movements displays any disquietude. Let this sorry enemy dare to rouseus, and they will find, at any hour of day and night, something to talk about! But we are learning to know them. Lazily the battleships and destroyers spread over the broad surface of the Adriatic and begin their majestic descent. This morning the cruisers were to northwards, in the vanguard. This evening they are deployed to the south, where their vigilance will win them some consolation for the afternoon.

Off Bari, 3 November;
four o'clock in the morning.

Thank God, I was on watch during the dark hours of the night. I should never have been able to abandon myself to sleep. For the disappointment of yesterday left me full of an exaltation there was no real battle to exhaust, and a thousand disconnected ideas raced through my brain. Even yet, after four hours of watching disturbed by alarms, I cannot find an instant of repose on my bed. I rise and come to talk with the confidante who is always ready, this notebook, which has received the confession of all my moods. Perhaps after this one-sided conversation my mind will become calmer and forget itself in sleep. But I am not sure. For we do not really know how to put ourselves to sleep.

I envy the soldiers on the solid land, confronting an enemy present before them. Whether he hides or reveals himself, the conflict is not slowin coming. They rush forward, they sing and shout; they thrust out their bayonets, they bite, and trample with their feet. At the moment of killing it is delicious to become a beast, to think no longer, to dry with a single gesture the sweat from one's brow, and the blood from one's wounds. But the sailors spend their energies in a long silent waiting. The more active they are, the more profound is their silence. The nearness of death makes them machines of precision.

I envy the soldiers who salute while charging their fallen enemy. They have seen him coming. Their short duel ends either in the intoxication of victory or the repose of death. Our long journeys are furtive steps in a temple of phantoms. Those who want to slay us crawl in the heart of liquid shadows. Those who defy us refuse an encounter, and entice us into the snares of the sea.

Night lags on the Adriatic. Nothing seems to live except our dreams. With elbows on the rail, eyes lost in the vastness, the officers of the cruisers keep somber and silent. Near their guns, motionless as statues sculptured out of shadow, the gunners watch in vain, and reflect on the disappointments of yesterday. In the distance there is a splendid thunderstorm. Forks of light leap from Italy to Austria; not a thunder peal echoes, but the air is alternately vivid and dark. The lightning comes and goes ceaselessly, like the winking of an electric giant. Black and white, white and black, the *Waldeck-Rousseau* glides through a gleaming sea. Are there enemies about us? Is the sea safe? How can our eyes tell, as they pass from an illumination whiter than the sun into an opaqueness blacker than nothingness? Every electric shock jangles the strings of our taut nerves. A reflection on the water takes the form of a destroyer; the straight path of the lightning shoots like a rocket of the enemy; the shadow has the thickness, the consistency, and almost the odor of smoke from a hostile ship.

O demons of the atmosphere, how you play with the sailors! Over there, towards the north, the watchers on the battleships have felt their hearts expand and contract with each of your shining caprices. But even greater is the disquietude of the cruisers who precede and protect the squadrons. Yesterday Austria saw us. In a grand gesture she refused us battle. To-night we feel it coming, we are sure of it. She has despatched her atrocious submarines. They blockade the Adriatic and watch for us. When shall we fall into their claws? In a minute, an hour, a day? We are illuminated like specters by every flash, but they are buried in the black waves. Both the cruisers and the battleships who trust themselves to our vigilance are lost in an ocean of illusion.

Early in the morning an ensign translates a wireless from Malta. By way of numberless cables this message brings news from the Pacific. Under the massive shadows of the Cordilleras of the Andes, three English cruisers were swallowed up in the Chilean twilight. They fought against stronger vessels, but the German guns *a eu raison de leur valeur*. Twelve years ago, from the height of the American peaks, I had looked over the infinite expanse where this passage at arms took place. A few years ago, during a cruise to China, I had visited these same British vessels. I remember their appearance; faces that smiled at me then are now, no doubt, sleeping over there on the threshold of the *madrepores*; fingers which pressed mine are twisting the dark sea-weed, the sailor's shroud. I envy those ships. I envy the dead of the battle of Coronel. A few weeks later, we shall know the details of their glorious end, but from now on I shall envy them, for they have fulfilled their destiny. It was not vainly that their torn flag shone in the sun. They struck, they perished, their eyes have carried with them into the deep the vision of battle; their death transmits a heritage of vengeance to which all British sailors are the heirs.

Why does fate give us in the Adriatic a felon enemy that only runs away? Certainly I hate the Germans; but at least you find them when you look for them. Whereas to draw from thedepths of the sea the only adversaries that Austria sends against us we should need picks and rakes. Our magazines are full, our engines are quivering, our guns thrust out their jaws, but all that crawls in the Adriatic desert is the submarine.

Silent lightning flashes, alternate shafts and shadows burn our eyelids. The four hours of the watch pass. My eyes are fixed on the blackness; my dreams encircle the earth every moment. A procession of memories has accompanied the storm. Perfumes from Indo-China, the theaters of Paris, negresses of Guadeloupe, Madagascar cyclones, idylls of the West and tragedies of the East, tropic homesickness, and the English countryside—the whole procession of the past glides through my watch. Smiling, mystical, dim, it hastens to respond to my mood of nervous fatigue. It leaps upon the bridge to companion my solitude. About all my comrades, about the officers, who like me have become hermits of the deep, there crowds in the same way the phantoms of the past. We do not summon them. They run to us, form in line, yield place to others; the train of our dreams is more mobile than the sea. Meanwhile duty does not suffer. The round of memories never deflects our eyes or our ears from the surface of the waters. When necessary, we can scatter the memories with a single gesture, and do whatever is needful.

In the freshness of the early dawn the breath of the breeze calms all this fever. My mind pauses on the last rung of the ladder of memory. There it rests, and at the end of my watch I find myself back again in a garden of Malta. According to the calendar this episode dates only eight days back, but it seems to me that our life has thrown it into the remote past.

In the midst of the arid rocks of Malta there is a garden, enclosed with high walls. The parterres of black soil, imported from Sicily, are cut by alleys of gravel. On the terrace bloom the rarest flowers under the sun. They are not European, they are choice specimens from America and Asia. The corollas which grow in this garden come only from certain Southern archipelagoes, but human skill has made them live in Malta.

Arbors shelter benches of ancient stone. Here and there arches of perfume brush the dreamer's head. Since it is a place of quiet and sovereign beauty, human beings do not frequent it. Every evening, before returning to the noisy streets of Malta, I spend a few solitary hours in the company of the flowers. Only the gardeners disturb my revery, but they early become acquainted with me. The third evening one offered me the bouquet that still perfumes my cabin, and refused my grateful reward.

That evening I was walking at the end of the garden, by a fountain with a brim of stone andtwo basins of green water. In it the twilight reflections dissolve. The fragrance that lingers there is enchanting. On this little lake float two white swans. They know that their prison will never be larger; the paddles of their feet are still; their dazzling wings, rose-tinted in the setting sun, open like a sail to the breaths of the breeze, and they glide very gently, bending their necks as if to breathe in the exquisite sweetness of the evening.

A little dog, tawny and silken, ran around the fountain, barking at the swans when they skirted the rim, at their disdain when they moved towards the center of the pool. On a bench a woman dressed in mauve was reading a book, turning the page slowly. The air held only the last vestiges of light. When this woman raised her attentive eyes towards the dog, she revealed a sorrowful face and eyes heavy with passion.

I am slightly disturbed by these neighbors, but I sit down and abandon myself to the witchery of the colors and odors of the dying day. Sorrow is solaced by an excess of sorrow, and the exile finds joy only in an excess of exile. Solitary, between the past and the future, I am at peace.

There in the fragrance of the garden, the sea, the war, the how and why of things, all disappear. My thoughts float, without support, like the exhalations of flowers which hasten to give out a sweet odor before falling asleep. But the littletawny dog, excited by the play of the swans, leaps towards the nearest ones, and falls into the water. He keeps himself up, paddling round in the same place; he scratches at the slippery rim of the fountain. Unable to climb out, he whines piteously. I fish him out by his silky ears. He shakes himself, shakes water on my shoes, and the lady in mauve rises to thank me.

Who ever remembers words spoken at twilight? She spoke the soft Italian tongue, and I replied in kind. Why, as I came from the shores of Malta, should I forget French in favor of the tongue of Dante and d'Annunzio? The little tawny dog followed us. I learned that he is called Jimmino.

Deep eyes, a face which was not pretty but which I thought to be more beautiful than beauty, was sometimes raised to mine. We walked along together, both weary. Our words were vague, and yet each one found its mark. I understood my own fatigue; but what was this woman's with the tragic face? We had not told each other our secrets, and yet it seemed that for each other we had no more secrets. She was beautifully dressed, in rare and simple material. Her jewels were real. Night had enveloped us when we reached the gates of the town. You wish to know what we said to each other on the way? I do not remember. Under an electric light in the street, we pressed each other's hands; her eyes dominated her pale face, and I thought her fingers trembled. Who is this passer-by whom perhaps I shall never see again, and will she take her place in the company of the shadows who people the life of the sailor? I do not even know her name.

On the bridge my successor in the watch comes to replace me.

"Speed, twelve knots," I say to him. "Route, to the south. We have passed the light at Bari. Range of the guns, fifteen hundred meters. Deflection, forty-four and fifty-six. Light wind from southwest. Storm continues on the whole horizon. Nothing in sight. A good watch to you!"

And I go down to my cabin. Perhaps after two hours of confession on paper, I shall find oblivion for this chaos in which my dreams are tossed. But I must sleep, for in six hours I stand watch again, and the folly of the mind must not be allowed to weaken the body.

3 November,
four o'clock in the afternoon.

Well, no! Sleep did not come this morning, and all these dreams came near ending in a fatal nightmare.

After a few hours of unquiet rest, I had to rise, make a hasty toilet, and swallow what food I could before resuming the lookout. In the middle of the day I found myself on the bridge I had left in darkness a few hours before. The sea was silvery in a bright sun. In a spreading line the three cruisers continued their course towards the southern end of the Adriatic. Behind us, almost invisible on the horizon, the smoke of the "naval army" made a black smudge. On board, everyone not on watch was taking a siesta, getting consolation in sleep for the disappointments of the preceding day. But dozens of eyes were watching this calmest of seas. Light mists, idle as the feathers of birds, moved here and there on the blue sea. A few thousand meters away the *Ernest Renan* followed a parallel course.

Suddenly in the streaks of foam appeared something whiter. My glass at once followed this wrinkle on the water; one would have said it was a jet of steam, glistening in the sunlight. I hesitated a few moments. Perhaps I had been deceived by the fin of a porpoise swimming at the surface. But the memory of drills during peace-times set before my eyes the wake of a periscope, and I hesitated no longer.

"On watch! To port! Range, eight hundred meters! Deflection, forty! The three engines ahead full ahead! Close the port stanchions! Open fire!"

The cruiser leaps. Below, the men on watch close the port stanchions. The volley of guns goes off, and the shells fall round that white moving spot. They burst like balls of snow on a blue wall. All the men wake from their siesta, the officers come on deck. At several meters fromour hull passes the flaky line of a launched torpedo. It has missed us, but a big 194 shell, fired from one of our turrets, bursts just above the periscope, which rises, sinks, rises and sinks again, like a wounded animal which lifts itself and falls back. And then we see nothing more. The blue water shows only its usual indolence. From the *Ernest Renan* comes to us a burst of hurrahs across the air; they have seen the shell tear up the water, and have decided that the explosion destroyed the submarine.

We move rapidly, so rapidly that in a very few moments the cruiser is far away from the deadly spot. The guns turn and follow, ready to fire again, but nothing more appears.

"Cease fire! Watch ended! Open the port stanchions! Return to course! The three engines at sixty revolutions!"

In a few seconds the cruiser resumes its watch. It has just proved that it cannot be caught napping, and everything falls back into what appears to be somnolence, but a somnolence with eyes wide open. Have I sunk an Austrian submarine? I shall never know. This deceitful enemy that hides itself to strike, and hides itself to die! One at least will not attack the precious battleships which follow us.

Towards the east a few minutes later the *Jules Ferry*, a cruiser with four stacks, which has been reconnoitering on the other side of the horizon,signals that a torpedo from an invisible submarine has passed a few meters from its hull. So there were at least two of these invisible enemies, and it was the cruisers that baffled their attempt. The Commander-in-Chief can descend fearlessly the path which we have just swept clear.

What does one feel on learning in the space of less than a minute that a cruiser worth fifty millions and carrying a thousand men has been dependent for life on the promptness of an order or the intelligence of a maneuver? I know nothing about it, and all those who have known great responsibility in this war will understand what I mean. A little later on, it seems to me, one feels afraid of the peril that is now past. It presents itself under terrifying colors which in the moment of action one did not see at all. Courage is easy enough; you need only get out of yourself, think of others, and everything becomes simple. Afterwards you are much fatigued. After yesterday's disillusionment, I doubted my being able to sleep. To-day, after this danger, I am sure to escape insomnia. The phantoms of the past will not knock at the door of my memory, for I have lived through a great moment of my life. I may have saved the *Waldeck-Rousseau*!

Otranto Canal, 11 November.

Outside or near the shore, in a peaceful harbor or in a roadstead whipped by the winds, a navalcollier speaks the *Waldeck-Rousseau*. For several hours coal by the hundreds of tons passes from the collier to the ship. After so many days of watching and weariness, and of stoking the fires, this is the rest which our crews taste. We coal in front of Corfu or Paxo, or in some cove of Epirus. Each week our insatiable furnaces demand a thousand tons of coal; each week we burn them up in our futile promenades across the Adriatic sea.

From dawn to dusk our sailors fill sacks in the bottom of the collier's hold; their shovels and picks labor in the bosom of the black stuff; windlasses raise the clumps of sacks, and cast them on the deck. There other gangs take charge, lower the sacks by chutes into the bowels of the *Waldeck*, dragging them by hand through the labyrinth of passageways, and into the gaping jaws of the stores; at the edge of the store-room two men with powerful muscles turn out with one stroke a hundred kilos of coal which fall down into the darkness amid a cloud of blinding dust. Crouched at the bottom of the store-room, other sailors receive this dark avalanche, pouring minute after minute; they direct it, pile it up in empty corners, and, stumbling on the piles, their eyes burned by the tar, their mouths poisoned with soot, prepare the way for the new torrents which are coming.

You would imagine yourself in a cavern of theinfernal regions. Around the cruiser and the collier a thick halo sullies the atmosphere. Bound together by heavy hawsers, the two boats roll on the waves or in the wind like two black swans. On the decks and broadsides you see only dark forms which move with sluggish gestures; bare feet travel furtively the carpet of coal spread over the steel; electric lights under a black film throw a strange and somewhat sinister light; human beings pass, loaded with heavy sacks, knees bowed, eyes and teeth white in a perspiring negro mask; they pant and blow and suffer. Their muscles are aching with this work fit only for horses, and beg for mercy. Yet they sing. At the moment when the cloud is heaviest, the odor most acrid, and the light most livid, a hoarse young voice rises out of the gloom. It attempts the first verses of some gay song: "The Young Girls of Rochelle!" "Queen Pomare!" "The Gray Lark!" Right and left, high and low, invisible singers respond. The coalholes become alive; behind the partitions of steel a smothered baritone joins its raucous tones to those of a tenor armed with a pick. And in the immense maze of the holds, the broadsides and corridors, flows a harmony, at once sad and joyous, a memory of France in days of peace. There is no conductor and no metronome, but the singing is in good time and tune. The cruiser vibrates in unison with it.

When the song is ended, one hears for several minutes only indistinct breathings and stampings. Sack by sack the tons of coal stock the holds, and the monotonous rain accompanies the interminable labor.

For Nature begins to grow somber. The worst weather has not come yet, but the sky suggests the melancholy of winter; the South Wind sometimes gives place to the North Wind, and we have bitter hours. Then the coalings are unspeakably dismal; our beautiful cruiser is clothed in a dusty cloak which trails over her hull like a mourning mantle; the smoke from the stacks mingles with the gusts of coaldust which the wind and rain plaster over the guns, the cordage, and one's own skin. Floods of despair seem to descend from the clouds.

To chase away these evil impressions we go to talk with the Captain and the officers of the collier. They come from Cardiff or from Newcastle, are familiar with the ports of England and France, have seen our French comrades and the British fleets; they bring us news of the vast world. We listen to them eagerly. They too belong to the great fraternity of navigators, and the tales they tell us are like the Odyssey we live. Up there, far up, between Norway and Scotland, the English cruisers are keeping indefatigable watch, and they are less fortunate than we. For there the sea is sinister. Around England, without pause or respite, in terrible storms, the Allied destroyers prowl everywhere. Covered with spray, laboring through the fog, they contend with the sea without meeting any other enemy; and the fleet of Admiral Jellicoe dances attendance like our own "naval army!" Ignominious and cowardly, the German enemy hides himself, just as here the Austrian burrows away. The proud descendants of Nelson await a new Trafalgar, and to them the prudence of the Germans opposes only hidden enemies, the submarines. As for our French brothers, the destroyers and Atlantic cruisers, they journey from Calais to Brest without adventure; convoyers of transports, policemen of the waves—customs-officers of contraband, they do not experience the excitements of the Adriatic hunts. Their task, more obscure than ours, is also more ungrateful. And since the happiness of man is measured by the unhappiness of others, we are happy in the Adriatic in spite of our disillusion and our exile.

But the day passes. The Captain of the collier offers us the latest papers, we give him the last wireless messages, and we must separate. Whether or not the coaling is ended, the cruiser never stands still during the night. We cast off the hawser, the screws turn; the crew, black with coaldust, go to rest their weary limbs after the crushing toil of the boilers, the engines, and the watch.

And during the rest of the night the cruiser makes a hundred or a hundred and fiftymiles. It matters not whether the sea is calm or disturbed, the sky clear or rainy. Men and officers observe the same vigilance as they did yesterday and will to-morrow; every boat that is sighted is chased, stopped, visited; one takes no account of weariness or sleep. One goes steadily on, always steadily on.

And if the thousand or twelve hundred tons necessary are not taken on in a single day, we return next day to the collier. The rendezvous is not at the same place, but in quite a distant roadstead or bay, for fear that the enemy, forewarned, will send us a submarine while we are practically helpless. In all haste we finish emptying the coal; the holds are full to the jaws, the sailors take courage and forget their weariness in a supreme effort. We fortify ourselves again for eight or ten days, for the excitements of the Adriatic, the dangers of the sea and the torpedoes.

Everything is impregnated with coal. There is no barrier or filter against this microbe. Bathing in floods of water, brushing and scraping does not chase it from its lairs. In our food our teeth encounter crunching lumps; our hair is tarnished with a black cosmetic; and the folds of our whitest linen conceal little hoards of soot. Our whitest linen! Is there a world where they know the pleasure of immaculate shirts? Of handkerchiefs pure as snow? When we set out, each one of us took along only what was strictly necessary. Ourboxes are few, and in a day we soil more than in a week of peace. Where are the washes of other days? where the polite laundresses of the ports, who washed the linen and cambric in twenty-four hours? Our cruises last eight or nine weeks.

How many times already I have washed in my basin two handkerchiefs and a shirt so covered with coaldust that the white places spotted it! Like all my comrades I have a sailor at my service. But he is a good gunner, who only looks after me when his duties do not call him elsewhere. Every day he has ten hours of lookout and three or four of preparation of materials. Must he not sleep and eat? When he is free, I try to take a few hours of broken rest on my bunk, and he respects my sleep. When my cabin is empty, he is watching behind his gun. Each one of us washes what he can. The soft water we use does not come from clear fountains, but from the boiler tubes which distil the sea-water; it stands in great metal casks, it is filled with rust and retains the color of it. In vain we throw in soap and borax; the washed linen turns yellow as if powdered with mustard, and it is never quite dry. The falling rains, the smoke which sweeps the deck, do not permit hanging it outdoors. In my cabin my gunner has stretched two strings between the port hole and the moulding above my bunk, and up there the linen dries as well as it can. Sometimes, while I sleep or work, an idle drop falls on myface or my paper; other times the constant vibration of the cruiser throws the linen to the coal-stained linoleum, and the whole thing has to be done over again. In the "naval army," as in the trenches, nothing is clean but the wind.

As in the trenches, too, we try to kill time, which lags so terribly. The study of the military map is misleading; we are accustomed, as each communiqué is received by wireless, to stick flags on the Western and Eastern fronts. The pins change every day by a quarter or a tenth of a millimeter; they have made so many holes in the paper that one can no longer read the names, and we have given up taking them out. Bundles of papers arrive in each mail, are quickly read and thrown aside; they feed neither our conversation nor our reveries. We brought no books from France because we thought them superfluous in a short war, and those we have ordered for these interminable cruises have not yet come. Letters are quickly written when one has nothing much to say and the censor forbids details.

What have we to do except play? Some spend their hours off in Patience; it is all one to them whether the combinations come out or not. Others bend over the chess-board, or become absorbed in bridge. But these are unusual kinds of chess and bridge; no one ever has time to finish a game. The service, the watch, meals, the time for sleeping, interrupt you; you leave the chess game orthe rubber where it is, and another officer takes your place. A game commenced with certain partners ends with a completely new set. Winning or losing does not matter; one has time only to kill, and must think of nothing else.

Adriatic Sea, 16 November.

For several weeks now the monotony of our vagabondage has been broken by a pleasing distraction—divine service celebrated every Sunday. For the duration of the war the Government has appointed on every admiral's ship and every hospital ship a volunteer chaplain. Ours arrived the middle of October. His name is Mgr. Bolo.

Without regret he has left his care of feminine souls, his delightful home in Touraine, and has sought the hard life of the sailors. After a long voyage he appeared at some bay in the Ionian Isles where we were coaling, and climbed the iron ladder of our ship in the thick of the rain and soot. For several days, while he was bewildered by the mazes of the cruiser, or breathless in his stifling cabin, he might have wondered into what world he had got. But a serene soul dwelt in his athletic body; he quickly got over his confusion, and in order to preach better to the sailors, he wanted to learn their trade.

He is constantly asking questions; our jargon, the complicated machinery, its mechanism and control, do not repel him. His talk is enlivenedwith racy words; in him the sailors recognize a brother. He is one of the crowd. Although his hands are accustomed to priestly gestures, he takes part in the embarkations. Each time we put the gig or long-boat in the water, he takes his place beside the coxswain and tries to direct the crew. He soon learned the usual orders, how to manage the sail and the oar, and how to make a difficult landing or tack. In a few weeks he could safely be entrusted with the direction of a ship's boat in all the difficulties of current, wind and waves; he directed it with confident voice and hand. Then we made him undergo the same examination as the able seamen, and if it would please him to have the title *in partibus*, we will deliver to him the certificate which will make him a real priest-sailor.

During the cruises he tries to pierce to the soul of that mysterious race, the sailors. For those who have preached to country and city folk the task is not easy. The sailors, artless and at the same time instructed by their travels, used to danger and to duty, do not take to specious rhetoric or childish advice. Hyperbole and platitude displease them equally. They have minds like the fishermen and workingmen whom of old John the Baptist or Jesus persuaded. One must search their heart rather than their reason, their imagination rather than their intelligence. In this way the preaching may bring them some simple truths, admonish their rather loose impulses, and give them resignation for their fatiguing tasks.

Every Sunday religious service is held on board; it is a simple and dignified ceremony. Around the portable altar, the flags make stained windows; the arch of the church is replaced by the low whitewashed ceiling between decks; to right and left the partitions of the cabins, the white bodies of the stacks form the metallic walls of our temple; variegated funnels, valves, well-polished faucets, throw out sparkling reds and yellows; chairs for the officers, benches for the crew, cover eight or ten meters of the space. Anyone who wishes attends. A bugle call announces the Mass, and anyone not on duty may be present or may excuse himself. While the priest recites, one hears the respiration of the engines below, the snorting of the ventilators; overhead on deck tramp the sailors of the watch; the great waves of the Adriatic slap against the hull, and the quiver of the moving ship makes the altar tremble. Now and then there is music, old liturgic airs and modern themes.

The priest addresses the sailors. He does not need to teach them heroism, to make fine phrases. The instinct of the sailors is surer. They are convinced by eternal truths, discussed with sincerity. Our Bretons, our Provençals, listen receptively to the gospel of the day. When they hear simple words, like those the Galilean used two thousand years ago, their lips are parted, their deep eyes become absorbed, their souls grow better. But if they hear argument, they make an effort to understand, they knit their brows, they discuss within their own minds. They reflect what is good and clear and simple; one is sure to touch them when one seeks their hearts.

The *Domino, salvam fac rempublicam* is played. The priest passes between the rows on his way to his cabin, and the congregation disperses. Five minutes later, benches and flags have disappeared, the place has recovered its solitude and its calm. The sailors before the engines or behind the guns remember with pleasure what they have just heard. Believers or not, they know that sincere words have been spoken and yield themselves to their influence.

Thus, in early ages, in the clearings or the fields, the apostles must have preached to rude peoples. They sowed the seed that ripened throughout the centuries; their temples were no more splendid than this steel vessel which spends every Sunday traversing the sea.

Near Santa Maria de Leuca,
17 November.

We have on board an eye which never sleeps; it is the wireless. Its apparatus is buried in the depths of the ship; a cabin hung with mattresses isolates the operators from the noise of the engines, and the general confusion. The telegraphers listen to messages from every direction; the lowest murmurs of the electric voice do not escape their ears.

The air vibrates continually. From stations far and near, from ships sailing the Atlantic or nearer waters, the calls and messages find their way; the air carries them instantaneously. The powerful poles of the Eiffel Tower, Ireland, Germany, Italy, Constantinople, overcome the fainter messages. They send out to any distance, with all their force, the official news of the conflict. If someone else is speaking too loud five hundred or a thousand kilometers away, they increase their current, swell their voices, until these interlopers are silent.

There is a certain tacit agreement about their transmission. Germany does not interrupt France; the Turk waits until Malta has finished; Madrid, talking with Berlin, ceases when London speaks. For these great stations, controlled by the Governments, send out only the more important messages, those which the entire world ought to hear; they wish neither to be confused nor to confuse others. Communiqués from the front, events at sea, diplomatic or financial transactions, apologias or recriminations, circulate in all languages. One can be sure the papers will not publish them. If by chance the reader finds them in his daily newspaper, it will be a week or two later, under some disconnected, unrecognizable form.

The sailors, however, get all the news. While the censor limits the rest of the world to meager and belated information, we know it all already. We can rejoice or mourn in advance of the rejoicings and grief of millions. Ireland announces a simple strategic movement of the Russians, but Norddeich—the German station—echoes everywhere the claim of a German victory, with an advance and the taking of thousands of prisoners. Norddeich relates briefly some happening at sea, but Eiffel makes her most powerful sparks crackle as she sends to Moscow, to Terra Nueva, to the Soudan and the Red Sea, the news of a naval disaster to some German ships. How soon and in what distorted form will the public read this news? At every hour of day and night we receive the messages, brutal and imperious.

We cannot be deceived. Even our enemies take no pains to prevaricate in these messages to ambassadors, consuls, and their innumerable agents who uphold German prestige throughout the world. It is of the utmost importance for Germany that these men receive honest information with which to make a case for their negotiations. There is nothing in common between the rhapsodies of the papers or the Wolff Agency, and its wireless information. At the most, in the case of defeats, it carefully renders a vague account. But this vagueness makes us prick up our ears, and in a few hours London or Paris confirms the English or French victory.

Outside of chancelleries and Government offices there are no maps kept up to date except those on ships of war. In the ward-room we argue over the flags that are placed at the precise spot where they should be; our predictions and our hopes are rarely deceived. And if secrecy did not bind us to silence, we could tell our friends much news.

But underneath these important voices of the wireless are whispers of many lesser tones, just as in the tropical forest the roaring of the lions does not silence the sounds of insects and rodents; this undertone of smaller voices is what gives the jungle its deep voice. The thin voices of the ships that speak to us give the sea air a mysterious animation. A great liner on its way from tropic seas announces its passage by some frequented cape. A torpedo-boat on patrol near Gibraltar tells Port Said of the ships it has sighted. This torpedo-boat's apparatus is not powerful enough to call the other end of the Mediterranean; it signals Bizerta or Toulon, which answer it, take its message, and send it like a ball rebounding on the stations at Malta, on the masts of a French cruiser in the Ionian, on the wires of a Russian ship in the Ægean Sea, until it finally reaches the station at Port Said. A mail-boat gives information about its position; a squadron asks for orders; a naval attaché or ambassador sends word about espionage; the Resident General at Morocco is sending grain to Montenegro; the patrols warn of a submarine in sight; colliers ask us to tell them where they will find certain battleships: the whole Mediterranean knocks at the wireless station of the Commander-in-Chief, like a crowd of subalterns at the door of the officer who is giving out orders.

And the Commander-in-Chief on his splendid battleship—a moving office—decides, orders, directs; the sonorous rays shoot out from the mast where floats his flag that represents France, and through space, far and near, through the stations which relay them farther on, travels their echo to the ear of the recipients.

There is no disorder, no discord, in these messages. Just as with the players in a well directed orchestra, all the speakers speak on the minute, at the very instant they should; watch in hand, the telegraphers wait for their moment, and at the highest speed send their dashes, short and long; at the end of their period whether they have finished or not, they stop and wait, for immediately a distant voice begins to play its tune, and would complain violently if someone prevented its talking. The Mediterranean is divided into sectors, and the time distributed between them, so that no one is allowed to speak if the schedule requires him to be silent.

Offenders, moreover, are soon recognized. Just as the finger of a blind man acquires surprising sensibility, the telegraphers come to know the timber, sharpness of tone and musical richness of these babblers they have never seen. For the initiated the electric radiations have a personality like human talk. Two stations, two ships, have distinct voices and deliveries. This one sputters, that one speaks slowly and gravely; the sound of one resembles a match struck on sand paper, another buzzes like a fly, another sings sharply like a mosquito. It is a magic concert. In his padded cabin the receiver hears and makes out the whisperings of the grasshopper, the scrapings of violins, the rattle of beetles, the frying of boiling oil, all the sounds which the fantastic electricity reproduces hundreds of miles away. It jumps, stops, recommences; one would call it a symphony of goblins in a boundless land. And yet the least of these vibrations is a messenger of war, of life, or of death.

They are careful to use secret languages. There is not a word or phrase in this continual interchange which anyone could interpret without the keys upon which depends the safety of the ships. Nothing but cipher circulates through the air. All the combinations which the human mind could invent, all the ingenuities devised by specialists, have been prepared beforehand. We improve on the arrangements of ciphers; for fear that the enemy, after receiving pages and pages of ciphered texts, will succeed in forcing the lock, the "naval army" does not long maintain the same keys. It modifies them, turns them about, rubs them down; and the officers in charge of the translation are like travelers who change languages at every frontier.

Furthermore, everyone does not speak the same language; sometimes they address one another without anyone's being able to understand. From Englishman to Englishman, Frenchman to Frenchman, minister to admiral, admiral to cruiser, commander-in-chief to the least of his satellites, ambassador to battleship, consulate to shore station—between these leap dialogues in unknown patois. The curious can listen, but they will learn nothing. As worthy descendants of the Gauls, whom Caesar describes as stopping travelers en route to get news from them, we are all eager to know the message of the ciphers which we read without our codes' being able to interpret them. Labor lost! Perhaps one of us has patience, enough, or works long enough, to decipher a secret not meant for him. He is happy. He acts important. He thinks he is very superior to have known how to listen at the keyholes. But some fine day the key whose secret he has learned becomes useless in his hand; it gives him only words without order, nonsense. The two talkers have amused themselves with changing the lock, and everything has to be done again. The naval allies dread enemies with ears that are too wide open as much as indiscreet friends with too long tongues. And it is a good thing they do.

Besides, we have enough to do in translating the intelligible messages. In addition to the lieutenant of the chief vessel of the patrol and the chief of the watch and his second, there is a fourth officer who spends his whole time looking over files of texts received by the wireless. At his side are codes and dictionaries containing every word, phrase or signal which he needs to know. He spends four hours translating the numbers into French. English, Russians, French, Montenegrins, Serbs, all have something important, something vital, to say. During the day a hundred or even two hundred telegrams arrive, and are transcribed in blankbooks; the sender, the destination, the number, the hour of transmission, are all carefully noted. These are the archives of our naval Odyssey.

A wireless is often addressed to the *Waldeck-Rousseau*. The station that is calling sends out into space the name of our cruiser. We respond. From shore and from the ships come unexpected instructions and questions. In the dark night we transmit to the Commander-in-Chief whatever message demands a reply. The Commander considers, weighs carefully the words which he will send back; the officer in charge of the translating writes it out clearly and concisely in cipher. And a few minutes later the masts of the ship flash out their long and short dashes into the midst of the darkness. It is the answer that we are sending. The wires stretched between the masts become phosphorescent, the sparks crackle drily, and instantaneously, at no matter what distance, the one who is calling us hears the faint echo of our voice.

Thus pass the days, vibrant with this invisible business. Everyone tells what he knows, listens to what he ought to hear, responds when he is called. From the ocean to the Red Sea, all the wandering ships are held together by these bands, and the magical electric current effaces distance. But there are times when one is silent.

When, on the trail of adventure, the bold vessels go up the Adriatic to the threshold of their enemy, their voices are as hidden as their path is dark.

However imperious the calls, they do not reply. All about them, at Cattaro, at Lissa, in the islands and arsenals, the telegraphic spies would hear their voices as they approached. Dark and silent, they move without speaking. All chinks are stopped up in the cabin where the men listen. All along the route, in these furtive hours, they catch mysterious conversations. Some Austrian spy in Italy or the Greek Islands has seen in the twilight the departure of the French fleet towards the north. In a chimney, or cellar or well, this spy has concealed a transmitting station of which the neutrals are ignorant; he sends brief messages which sound like a whistle. We do not understand the numbers, but we guess what they mean. "The French are about to leave," "they are leaving," "they are in the Adriatic," "they are approaching Cattaro." No French mouth is responsible for this hostile voice; we know it by its singing timber like a flute or a mosquito's buzz. It is the Telefunken apparatus which produces this sound, which one would recognize among a thousand. All night its vibration follows us. Whence come these whispers in the darkness? By what miracle, from moment to moment, do we hear these sonorous flashes which talk about nothing but us? "The French are passing Brindisi;" "they are passing Bari;" "they are turning towards the northeast;" "about two o'clock they will be near Pelagosa." In the distance vibrate the responses, which become more and more distinct. It is Cattaro, Pola, the Dalmatian Isles, awaiting us.

Yes, we move in a circle of sinister spirits, and these Germans have prodigious ears. Their high shrill murmur, undecipherable yet very clear, darts round us as we advance through the darkness. Perhaps destroyers and submarines are lurking on our course. Those that have missed us in our too rapid progress telegraph the next sentinel, and he rushes toward us with his torpedo ready. Where is he? Behind or in front? Gunners, do not sleep at your guns! Officers, bend over the empty blackness! Cruiser, enveloped in shadow, move faster and ever faster! These evil specters of the Adriatic are lying in wait for you; the whistling of their ghostly lips prepares your destruction! But do not be afraid. They will wear themselves out in the pursuit, and to-morrow you will be at the post where France desires you.

But what cruiser, which battleship, is destined to receive the fatal wound from these singing demons?

West of Corfu, 26 November.

The naval struggle in which the Germans pretended to imitate the great corsairs of France has ended with the destruction of the *Emden* by an Australian cruiser in the Bay of Bengal. The armed liners—the *Kaiser Wilhelm, Cecilie, Cape Trafalgar*, and many others—have already paid the penalty for their futile audacity. They thought they could terrorize sailors and starve out nations; but in fact the resources of life are going to flow more abundantly than ever into the markets of the Allies.

The navy is the guardian of the granaries. We already knew it who frequented the important routes in times of peace, but five months of labor have proved to us that we never realized its full significance.

We have seen pass us, and have protected, innumerable freighters loaded with grain for bread, with animals for meat, and steel for the manufacture of shells. The warships have freed the routes which supply our champions with food, and have closed up the routes of the enemy. How many months longer will this enterprise take? The lips of the future are sealed. But the cruisers and torpedo-boats, from Norway to the Ægean Sea, do not shrink from their task. A nation at war requires some of its defenders to labor in assuring a living to those who fight. The deeds of sailors are not brilliant and showy; and men are not grateful to them for their fatigue. What matter? If this obscure work of the ships keeps the tears of famine from being added to the grief of mourning, it will not have been without a glory of its own; the smiles of happy little children will be our reward.

But I am forgetting the *Emden* and the corsair liners. Like the sea my imagination is somewhat capricious. These restless corsairs are of a piece with the general parody which German Kultur offers us. What would the Jean Barts and the Duquesnes say to the bandits that are spewed forth from Kiel and Hamburg? In the great period of Dunkirk and Saint Malo, pirates attacked magnificent galleys, sailing before the wind to Spain and the Thames. Like the brave foxes they were, they reveled in bold and clever combat. They were the prodigal sons of the sea. They played an honorable game, and never took pride in mere blind massacre.

One can imagine how the terrors of the sea would have been increased if a few years more of peace had permitted Germany to forge new weapons. Of her liners and cruisers she has picked the most powerful and rapid, and has said to them: "Kill, sink, and fun away!" Nothing is sacred to the barbarians of Rheims and Louvain, neither cathedrals nor the routes of the sea. What would not have been the horrors of this privateering war if William II himself or one of his lieutenants had had control of these maritime massacres? Before them the grisly imagination of the Middle Ages would have paled. What crimes will the Germans not commit when they realize that they are conquered?

Honor to the officers of the *Emden*! They have destroyed ships, but they nobly refused to commit the crimes commanded by their master. They generously spared the lives of the sailors who were at their mercy, and blood does not dishonor the tale of their exploits. Doubtless the praise of blood has disgraced them at Berlin, but the fraternity of sailors does not condemn them.

England accepted the challenge. Over the vast expanse of ocean she deployed her cruisers, launched them forth on the path of the marauders, and ordered: "Suppress them!" No pardon, no weakness! The Emperor at Berlin had revived the law of blood; so one took vengeance on his satellites. They all disappeared.

The last victim, the *Emden*, suffered the doom which it had so often inflicted. It had hunted down twenty harmless steamers, and was then in pursuit of a British convoy. To-day, broken, lying on an Indian reef, it serves as a reminder to wandering sailors. First they will salute this heroic prow, which knew how to die and how to redeem its enterprise from ignominy. Then they will give thanks to the fate that had them born of another race than the German.

Strait of Ithaca, 30 November.

The Commander-in-Chief has ordered the *Waldeck-Rousseau* to leave its Adriatic station—Otranto, Fano, Albania—for an anchorage in the Ionian Isles at Arkudi.

We go a short distance out to sea before approaching the maze of islands. To the north disappear Corfu, Paxo, and Anti-Paxo; to the south rise Saint Maure and Cephalonia; the great wall of the Orient covers the east; all the landmarks of our course are slowly displaced, giving way to others.

The officers of the watch pore over the chart. This great white sheet with its fine print indicates the contours, the data, the dangers, the routes. To those who do not know how to read it, it is nonsense; but its marks are our gospel. By its fine and intricate lines we can foretell how easy our voyage will be and where the dangers lurk. We sometimes think of the mariners of old who had no other guide than Providence. Reading these charts we wonder whether these regions were loved or feared, and whether, before risking his life there, the pilot invoked Neptune or the Virgin of the Waves.

We to-day are not so uneasy. Sky and sea are smiling. There is something treacherous in those blandishments of Nature, which recall the delights of autumn and yet suggest the coming of winter frosts. Their last tenderness is fragile.

Here we are in the strait of Dukato, between Saint Maure and Cephalonia. It is a splendid boulevard. To the right, Ithaca, Ulysses' native land, lies reddish brown under the sun; to the left, lie jewels of rocks and liquid paths more delicate and beautiful than remote trails in the depths of woods; before us a cluster of islands with names from the musical language of the rhapsodists—

Arkudi, Meganisi, Astoko. And like a highly polished tapestry, the marvelous mountains tower above the water, blue and crowned with light. The sea has the hue of mother-of-pearl; the sky is pale, the islands are veiled in faint color; the gods have composed these tints, outlines and places into a perfect fairyland.

Space seems to have a divine soul, of unknown substance. The eyes are ravished, the blood exhilarated. When Homer sang the return of Ulysses, the Ionian gods gave him a flexible and sonorous language. That secret the men of our times have lost, they must pause feebly on the threshold of the inexpressible. Surely Ionia was the garden of the gods.

The cruiser, slender and swift, glides between these historic shores, which have seen the barques of the Achæans, the triremes of Rome, the Venetian galleys, the ships of the Crusaders and the feluccas of Barbary. In our wake have passed generations of pilots, who came from regions where the sea is evil, and who laughed with delight in this sailors' paradise. Why should they not all—poets or merchants, pirates or soldiers—celebrate these delights and long to remain here? Blundering through schoolbooks, I have hated the very name of Ithaca; I have cursed Olympia—when it was assembled in a detestable book. Since then I have seen all the most perfect skies; my eyes have exhausted the miracle of light. And yet it is here that I place the cradle of the gods. When the fancy came to them to descend to earth, where else should they have lighted but on majestic islet, like Juno on a steep bank made by Vulcan? Was it not in this fair atmosphere that Apollo shook out his radiant locks?

And is it not this sea that gave birth to Venus? How happy he would be who could catch the secret of the outline and color play on this sea? Her fish are more beautiful in tint and form than the loveliest animals. Her plants have a rich metallic luster, with lines and curves that no land plants approach. The men who frequent her, the cities she laves, are fortunate. All beauty comes from the sea; every vital germ has floated in her depths. And the subtle intuition of the race of Homer, who gave divine form to symbols, made the goddess of life and beauty spring from the Ionian waves.

Aphrodite! Triumphant, naked, I see you emerging from the transparent blue sea: you stretch your soft limbs under the caress of light. You open your enchanted eyes upon an earth where men, harassed by the ugliness of their souls and the futility of their labors, stretch their hands madly toward your eternal beauty! You go to meet them. It was here you made your first appearance on our earth. Blessed be the Greeks, your sponsors, who chose this cradle for you!

And at this moment, when yonder on the field of murder the German ruffians are trying to destroy everything that is beautiful, everything to which you have given birth, I understand more clearly the patrimony which the French are called upon to defend. O Aphrodite, you extend across the ages your protection to France, your child. From this spot have come that clear thought, that delicate feeling, that fertile vision, which you loved in the people who nourished you. As a humble defender of that beauty, born of the bridal of sea and sun, a Frenchman thanks you for what you have given him, for all that which is now in danger of destruction; he salutes you in passing, Ionian Aphrodite, and wishes he could see the very circle of gold where the Greeks have placed your birth.

Do not think it is the force of antique memory alone that has produced this adoration of mine. From the bridge where I am carefully guiding the cruiser through the windings Ulysses loved, I see on deck a thousand sailors, silent and attentive. They have stopped talking and laughing, and no longer turn their backs to the too familiar sea. To-day a great silence hovers over these Bretons, these Flemings and Provençals. In what naive way are they absorbing the beauty before their eyes? They are not acquainted with the poetry and the prose which have endowed me with this ancient heritage. There they are, however, with wide eyes, lost in admiration. Beauty could not be celebrated more significantly than in this stupor of theirs. Their souls, I imagine, imprisoned in dark dungeons, unconsciously regret the speed of our passage. Their emotions are profounder than mine; theirs rise from depths where are no words to translate the mystery. When you do not understand a thing, you discuss it; but you are silent when it is revealed. All the sailors are silent. Beauty has just made itself one of their souls' memories.

At sea off the Peloponnesus, 2 December.

After so many weeks of cruising, without contact with the world, we had hoped to enjoy a few days of rest at Malta, a favor which the Commander-in-Chief grants to weary ships. We cherished the illusion that he had had us come so that he might deliver his communications to us and send us quickly on our mission. But in the navy one must never hope unless one wishes to be deceived. Hardly had we arrived at the anchorage of Arkudi when the *Waldeck-Rousseau* was charged with an urgent mission on the other side of the Balkan peninsula, to Saloniki. Regretfully she takes the southern route, winds around Greece and the Peloponnesus, turns towards the north, and through the mazes of the Ægean Sea seeks the road to Thessaly.

Our faces and eyes begin to show their weariness. It is not without betraying the strain that the stokers before their furnaces, the engineers before their pistons, the gunner lookouts before their guns, have lived this interminable length of days and nights, alternating between heavy labor and broken rest. The air between decks becomes heavier and more stifling with each passing day; dust and heat lie over everything, and one is as weary after a heavy sleep as at night on a railroad train with all the windows closed.

Everyone wonders whether we shall ever have the pleasure of engaging these Austrians or Turks, who hide in corners out of reach and send only submarines against us. The submarines are there; they are everywhere, they are nowhere. We stretch out our arms in the empty air; we strain our eyes in looking for the hiding enemy; and suddenly into the side of the vessel passes the wound that has no mercy. And it all happens in silence, for the naval warfare of this age is dumb.

I should only be tedious if I told in detail all the vain pursuits of our chases in the upper Adriatic, of patrols by night, of the sunrise, the light, the dusk. The days stretch hand in hand in a gray undulating vista across the water, at the end of which vanish the last hours we passed in France.

The Commander-in-Chief has cheered our dejection. The mission which takes us to Saloniki will take us later to Marseilles. That at least is the hope contained in our instructions. And we will be allowed to take a rest while we are in France. Everyone builds visions, calculates the time, and persuades himself that the Christmas holidays will find him again with his family. Already fathers seem to be caressing the fair heads of their children before the fireplace, husbands and lovers are trembling with a grave joy at the thought of this homeward voyage, a simple enough episode in our vagabond career, but charged with emotion because of the suffering of yesterday and the dangers of to-morrow. No one, however, dares complete these castles in Spain; too many miscalculations have marked our existence, as it is. As for me, who for eleven years have passed no single Christmas Eve in France, can I believe that a freak of war will grant me this happiness denied me by peace?

While we wait, each turn of the screws takes us further from France. Sparta, Cythera, the Cyclades, Corinth and the Piræus; these are the names which the officer of the watch gives to the lands that in turn come to salute us from the horizon. At the end of the map are marked the Dardanelles and Constantinople, other boundaries of this world war. Our cruiser has left the regions of danger in the Adriatic, and advances as fast as possible towards the waspish Turk. We move among beautiful scenery. Our eyes seek out a lighthouse on some island of celebrated name; our lips pronounce the name of some cape which the poets have made famous; we maneuver our engines and helm in an archipelago of tabernacles: Cythera, the temple of Venus, and Delos, the homeland of Apollo; Sparta, with austere countenance, and Athens, the rose of antiquity. Why cannot the sailor enjoy this dry, pure December weather? Under his feet the noble cruiser quivers. During his lookout, he smokes a light fragrant cigaret, and his thoughts, fluid like these pale curls of smoke, in happier times would have drifted back to the legendary epochs of old. But no human evil darkens the shining skies. For Austrian or Turk we must not cease to watch. I do not dream of complaining of that, for undoubtedly these hours portend violent homesickness for me.

Gulf of Saloniki, 7 December.

According to the schedule of watches I am in charge of the entry into the Gulf of Saloniki. From two to six o'clock in the morning I have directed the ship in this funnel of water, without lighthouses, with treacherous currents, at the end of which lies the much coveted city, that apple of discord between the Eastern peoples.

A treacherous fog sleeps on the surface of the water and shrouds the shores. Above it the moon dominates the heights and sheds its idle sparkling rays on the snows of Mount Olympus, Pelion and Ossa. Between the mists on land and the starry mantle of the sky, these peaks, whitened by the snow and by the decay of their own glory, keep watch in the deep silence. They are the only guide of the sailor lost in the fog; the officer of the watch and the young midshipman who assists him do not take their eyes off these tutelary presences. It is very cold. Towards four o'clock a freezing wind blows from Thessaly, and sharpens the edges of the snow to shining razors. My hands freeze on the glasses, and my eyes shed tears under the north wind. But one must forget such miseries.

A faint paleness lingers in the East, and spreads over the sky to our right. Straight ahead appear low plains, dotted with fires. The dawn comes, a moment full of difficulty and danger. My midshipman and I steer the course among the shoals.

At the moment when the last tack opens before us the roadstead of Saloniki, my successor comes to relieve me. The sunrise has taken possession of our world; the marvel of an Eastern morning emerges from the shadows of the night. I go quickly and drink a steaming cup of coffee, and come on deck again, to admire as simple spectator the panorama which I approached as pilot.

A stretch of frozen water, girdled with sands and marshes, reflects an uncertain light. Our prow breaks a way through the film of ice and broken splinters fall back on either side, like the crackling of frying cakes. Towards the mouth of the Vardar, legions of birds are skating and tumbling on this crust in which their claws can get no hold—the tumult of their voices disturbs the peaceful morning: fluttering moorhens, raucous herons, ducks in triangular flocks, wake and swarm about; rose-colored flamingoes poise themselves, motionless and pensive, on their needle-like legs, only a few meters from our course.

As our cruiser, sparkling with dew and glistening in the cold, penetrates farther into the white fog, a town emerges from the vagueness. It is still swathed in its morning gauze, its base is plunged in the fog, but its minarets offer their heads to the tints of the sunrise. One by one they show their slender outlines; soon they can no longer be counted for they form a forest of columns over the city. Surrounded by massive towers, the walls of the fortified castle on the summit of the hill are bathed in light; and beyond, stretching to the horizon, a desolate plain without trees or houses carries the eye towards Serbia, Bulgaria, Greece, or the steppes of Turkey.

Our anchor falls, and tears the parchment of ice. At length, after so many miles and journeys, the cruiser halts. All Saloniki is smiling under the kiss of the sun. Close to the water, as along all the Mediterranean shores, the buildings on the quay show their black commercial signs, gold façades of moving-picture palaces, and the white stucco and marble of hotels and banks. The streets, like dark tunnels through the mass of houses, rise from the harbor and plunge into the tiers of Christian and Jewish walls, up to the heights of the great amphitheater, where are massed the light blue Turkish cottages, surrounded by cypresses and clusters of plane-trees.

An Orthodox basilica flaunts its humped dome; the synagogue, geometrical and ugly, seems to hide in a confusion of terraces; a Catholic church raises its cross on a stone abutment; and the fifty minarets, with their slender swelling and tapering tops, point upward toward Allah's heaven. To the left, above the harbor, are tall smoking chimneys of brick; these are the minarets of the new god, industry, who has come at last to take his place among the sleepy Orientals.

Since we carry the flag of war in neutral waters, our cruiser must act with great scrupulousness. Greece consents to observe toward our mission a courteous hospitality, and we are careful not to abuse it. Since the beginning of the war the *Waldeck-Rousseau* is the first belligerent vessel to anchor in this cosmopolitan roadstead. All the East shudders. From the Serbian and Turkish storm clouds come bursts of thunder. Envies, hatreds and hopes wait only the hour to explode; Saloniki is a crossway where all currents collide. The presence of French sailors on shore might excite unpleasant demonstrations; the officers of the cruiser and the authorities of the city agree in refusing permission to sailors and officers to land until new orders arrive. This restriction does not include couriers, or negotiators, who are protected by the diplomatic immunities.

And here we are, imprisoned only a few fathoms from shore. Weary with walking the steel deck of the ship, we were rejoicing at the thought of getting acquainted with softer ground. After the glittering sea our eyes longed for the peaceful sights of the streets or the fields. We abandon hope of these meager pleasures, and, like Tantaluses of the sea, try to satisfy ourselves with the attractions in the roadstead.

From morning until evening, and up to nightfall, the harbor caiques come out to the French ship, besieging her and trying to fasten to her. But the same orders which forbid our visiting Saloniki in turn forbid access to the ship. No cajolery softens the officials; they repulse the most impudent attempts; and the rush of the barques is broken against our armor-plate. These resemble the narrow caiques of Constantinople. The people are curious as only the Easterners know how to be; they come in little groups, not haphazard, but according to race, beliefs, or opinions. The different groups correspond to the diversity of the city, where under the same heaven the mosques, the temples, the basilicas and the churches, adore so many different gods.

Large numbers of Greek soldiers with tanned faces come to observe us. To free themselves from the menace of war, they have hired boats together and come out to see what sailors look like who for four months have followed this profession of fighting. Later in some village of Bœotia or Locrida, they will relate to a rural audience the talk they had with sailors from Cornouailles or Provence. But between these two tribes of simple souls there is no common language to make intelligible conversation. An animated pantomime—sounds, grimaces, smiles, which everyone understands—has to serve. A finger is pointed towards the Dardanelles or Constantinople; another indicates the Adriatic; some comedian from Marseilles cries "Pan! Pan!" and a Theban gunner answers "Boum! Boum!" Great shouts of laughter burst from them. Hearts, if not lips, speak the same language.

Hearing this wild laughter, a crowd of Turks in black jacket and spotless fez, come round us silently. Their caiques are polished and painted green. Formerly these men were masters in Saloniki, but German duplicity launched their country into an adventure which lost them their fortunes. To them our flag is accursed. If some Turkish mine, wandering from the Dardanelles, should rip open our hull before their eyes, I swear they would raise to Allah strident cries of gratitude. But they are helpless and morose.

Their spite is only increased by the attentions we get from the friends of France. Some Englishmen, for instance, with their short pipes between their teeth and their chests open under a soft shirt, row about in pirogues; their bright eyes admire the cruiser as an instrument of sport, and the sailors as men who play the game of death. Passing, they rest their oars in front of the officers, and shout a "Hip! Hip! Hurrah!" at once emotional and precise, just as they might hail some cricket or football team.

Pretty Greek girls, with pure profiles and sly glances, add smiles, showers of flowers, and the brilliance of their new gowns to the enthusiasm of the men;

as they leave, their gloved hands throw towards the cruiser kisses which they think are unperceived; but our glasses miss nothing.

Serbs with tragic faces, with sunken and burning eyes, come to get new courage from contact with the French Navy. At this very moment their country is prostrate before the Austrian. Our flag comes to tell them: "Do not despair!" and they respond to our friendly salutations with pale smiles.

Quite at their ease, some Russians push their way among the crowd of barques. Whether their territory be invaded or not, whether their troops advance or retreat in the varying fortunes of this war, the Russians suffer neither extreme anguish nor extreme joy. They are quite serene. A cloud effaces the sun, but does not extinguish it. A reverse may annoy Russia, but she can wait; her victories will be the work of time. With a grand viva on their white teeth they salute their comrades of the great war, and then stay still, smiling.

These vivas excite ferocious glares in many an eye. Crouched on the benches in the boats are old Ottomans of Bagdad, or Mecca, or Erzeroum, who are telling over a shining chaplet of coral or nuts. These men are incorrigible. From their half shut lids, between their full lips, they dart towards the *Roumis* looks of hatred and imprecations. They glide at a distance of several meters from us, and do not stop their boat. The glances we are exchanging with our friends are profound, and charged with significance; the Mussulmans turn their eyes away to pretend indifference, but their rage is betrayed in the movement of their fingers which miss several beads at a time on their rosaries.

And what of these swarms of Germans, merchants, spies or fomenters of trouble, who crowd into the boats and instal themselves under our guns, to study the cruiser and the sailors? Here are these smiling but shameless faces, their eyes hidden beneath round spectacles, with which Germany blinds the world. Some of them, accustomed to this work, photograph us, enumerate our guns, observe our system of surveillance and protection. Before evening, telegrams in cipher will carry to Berlin all this information. They do it without shame; their disdain insults us with its impunity. Is not our territory invaded? Are not our Russian Allies harassed in Poland? Did not the British fleet, only a month ago, lose ships like ours off the coast of Chile? Have not our Serbian friends been driven back by the Austrians. "Germany over all!" We hear the arrogance they do not express. One of them dares to throw on deck a newspaper written in French. Attracted by the language, a sailor brings us the paper. But it comes from the press of the Wolff Agency; quibbles, monstrous lies, written in a French that would make negroes laugh, are dished up to the Levantines by the Teutons. We do not even want to shrug our shoulders; that would make these Germans who are watching us too happy. One among us rolls the sheet into a ball and throws it into the water; our impassive glances pass over these Germans encrusted along our hull. But under our uniforms our hearts beat a little faster.

A new arrival distracts us from these unpleasant neighbors. The children of the French school, conducted by French monks, bring us their rosy faces. Instead of games in the schoolyard, they have been rewarded with a view of the great ship, the ship which brings into the harbor the majesty of the great unknown nation. The ancestry of these children is diverse; their parents were born in Armenia, in Syria, in Thrace or Macedonia, but the gentle hand of France has already moulded their minds. They laugh with pleasure, their eyes show animation and clearness, traits of French thought. They rise and sit down again, curious to see everything, disappointed in not coming aboard, boisterous and friendly. When they go back regretfully in the twilight, they crane their young necks after us for a long time, and suddenly their young voices chant a thin but touching "Marseillaise." Their voices are inharmonious, their feeling breaks the verses, but the distance and the hour give to the sacred hymn an unbearable beauty. Like a perfume from our native land it floats over the water, fades away in the setting sun, and over there near the jetties becomes so faint that we seem to be hearing across space the song of our soldiers crouched in the trenches.

At that moment the sun disappears, and the cruiser makes its customary evening salute. Two gun shots resound in the pure air; our brass band plays the "Marseillaise;" the entire crew, hats off, turn towards the flag, which slowly descends from the top of the mast, brushes the bridge and guns in passing, and the soul of its native land comes to rest softly on the steel deck. During the night hours this standard, rolled up, preserves the love of France in its folds, and to-morrow, unfurling them to the sun, it will make them float anew on the seas we sail. Every evening and every morning in the wandering life of the sailor, these religious moments bring together Nature and Country, the two eternities; more religious even to-day in the presence of a thousand witnesses who are deeply moved. Standing, uncovered, all our comrades turn their gaze towards the tri-colored symbol, tinted with the blood, the purity, the hope, of our native land. In fury our enemies turn their heads away. The colored flag descends gracefully, smiles at us, but sets the others at defiance.

The water, purple for an instant, darkens and freezes. Our steam cutters disperse the boats, for the *Waldeck-Rousseau* must be solitary through the night. In this country where so many thieves prowl about, vigilance must not be relaxed. The German boats do not want to go. We jostle them, chase them, and soon the spies' faces have been cleared away from the approaches of the ship.

The night lights are lit in Saloniki; its quays are blazing, its slopes are flaked with light; the highest mingle with the stars. Dark and silent, the cruiser takes up her sentry duty; the roadstead is fast asleep, and the cold gradually covers it with a new shroud. On board it seems as if everything slept too, but the eyes of the lookouts never close, and the flag of France can repose in peace.

Pointe Kassandra, 10 December;
On the Fight in the Falklands.

What a fine revenge! The German squadron was sailing down the American coast. In this vast ocean she thought she had realized the ambition of the Kaiser: "The future of Germany is on the sea!" Admiral von Spee, the herald of Teutonic glory, was unfurling in the harbors of Chile the standard he said was invincible when a telegram from Berlin recalled him, probably to the North Sea, in order to add the strength of his cruisers to that of the fleet at Kiel.

The *Scharnhorst*, the *Gneisenau*, and two small cruisers began to double Cape Horn. They cleared the spur of the American world. I myself long ago went through the tempests and frosts which must have enveloped the German squadron in these windy seas. She reached the Atlantic, and turned towards the north. On the map of the world the Admiral's pencil had traced the routes leading to the Antilles, to the Azores, to the United States, to Ireland, and the northern latitudes of Norway, en route for the tunnel of the German *chenaux*. Protected by the luck which had followed him from China and Tsing-Tao, he expected no disaster.

In the South Atlantic the British leopard had placed his paws on the Falkland Islands; he had been foresighted enough to store there immense reserves of coal. The *Scharnhorst*, the *Gneisenau*, and their companions, made for this valuable booty, which they counted on seizing and stripping; for the place is as lost on the ocean as a helpless vessel. The German sailors, as they approached, had all the pleasure of playing a legitimate bad turn on their enemies.

But the wrath of Britain had launched on the sea great cruisers armed with *fouet*. Their orders were to discover these malevolent beasts, to chase and to scourge them to death. From the Mediterranean and from the English coasts, their greyhounds started on the merciless hunt, and swept the ocean as with a rake. Every time they put into port, they filled their magazines, they listened eagerly to the news of the world, and sailed ever farther south. When they learned that their game had turned along the American coast, they prepared for the grand hunt, assembled, and anchored in the Falkland Islands, in order to coal by night and lose no instant.

How strange the fate of ships at sea! Twenty-four hours later, and the coaling would have been done!

In the dawn of the next day, the lookouts on the Falklands saw the columns of smoke from the enemy ships in the distance. They came on like a cyclone. Admiral von Spee on his bridge was already imagining the telegram which should announce to Berlin next night his extraordinary prowess. But from the islands which they thought were deserted, they suddenly saw emerge in the morning light the prows of the great cruisers with their powerful guns. He counted them. He recognized their strength. His signals ordered flight. But the English pack had sniffed blood, and until evening it ran and killed.

I have just read the respectful words which, like an epitaph, the London admiralty dedicates to their fallen enemies. Admiral von Spee has nobly ended a stainless career. Far away in the midst of the beauty of the Levantine, the officers of my cruiser at first rejoiced at the victory. Then they saluted him, for one does not need to know all the final details to respect an end so glorious as his.

The *Scharnhorst* and the *Gneisenau* were cruisers of our own class, enemies of our own design. Why did they not choose us, three ships with our six smokestacks apiece? The fight would have been glorious, and the glory to the French. Shall we never confront anything but a desert sea, or invisible submarines?

Mediterranean, 13 December.

Our mission is ended; we are going not to France but to Malta. The Cassandras were right, and this twelfth Christmas holiday I shall pass where.... Courage and patience! Our comrades in the trenches are suffering in the slime and mud. We are commencing to freeze on a sullen sea. Winter will be hard for all the sons of France.

For several days the *Waldeck-Rousseau* has displayed the flag along the Levantine coasts. It has proved the vigilance of our country and her attention to the great cataclysms which are preparing in the East. It has encouraged the neutrals and informed the Turk that his turn will soon come. The cruiser has anchored nowhere. Her elegant outline passed far from islands or coasts, and the people who observed the smoke from her six stacks, could prophesy the future from the sight.

One morning we crossed the bay which is bordered by three nations, Turkey at Gallipoli; Bulgaria at Dedeagatch; Greece at Kavalla—respectively hostile, doubtful, friendly.

Gallipoli: a rugged mountainous peninsula, looking like Corsica. Behind its heights winds the passage of the Dardanelles, the path to Constantinople. For the moment this approach is forbidden us, and our guns quiver in vain. France and England wait their hour; the punishment of the Osmanlis will come later.

Dedeagatch: a seaport which Bulgaria conquered in the recent war. It is a badly situated harbor on an unfavorable coast; it seems to be surrounded by a desert; we can see immense freshly plastered barracks. A prize of war, it is filled with armament; as a maritime station it receives naval contraband for the Balkans. How many ships have we not halted who gave this port among their stopping-places? Our suspicions were rife; we saw that through this port the Turks were kept supplied. But Bulgaria remained neutral, the ships' papers had all the proper endorsements, and we had to let them pass.

Kavalla, Thesos and Samothrace: Greek harbor and islands. At the first the dissatisfied Bulgarians cast envious looks; they are inconsolable at having lost it at the same time as Saloniki. It is one of the bones of contention in an East which will never end its disputes. The name of this city will be famous before the war is ended. It was in the bosom of Samothrace that connoisseurs of sculpture found the statue which is the pride of the Louvre. In Paris at the head of a staircase, the perfection of her draped figure, with its graceful stride, delights the crowds who come to see her. She symbolizes Victory. For having placed her in the temple of her masterpieces, France deserves to add a jewel to the crown of this same Victory. She will not fail to do so. Our wistful thoughts pass to the violet rocks where the Victory slept under the earth, waiting so many centuries until she should awake in a French museum.

All these visions fade. Others succeed them, and each one brings a new dream. On a heavenly evening, one of the last fine evenings of the closing year, the cruiser passed Mount Athos, that jewel of the Christian faith. Her slopes are like a splendid robe sown with gems. The huts of hermits and solitaires cling to the sharp edges that the vultures and the eagles love. The pious men, who pass their lives preparing for eternal bliss, spend here their austere days, made fragrant with prayer.

Lower down, the convents form a ragged girdle; soft colors, blue, rose and faded green, give a religious tint to the walls; men, clothed in black—to represent the mourning for earthly passions—pray there for the sins of the world; they live on another planet, and the clamors of the world die at the foot of their sanctuary.

Before these priests and seminarists our smoking cruiser passes like a comet which comes from the unknown and goes into the infinite. The priests of Mount Athos salute us; they send up rockets, pale in the twilight; they set off firecrackers and Bengal lights, and perhaps their united voices send us an affectionate welcome. But the maritime comet passes; the noises reach it faintly, as the voices of men must reach the celestial altitudes.

Around a little cape appear huge convents, with sparkling gold domes. They are beautiful and desolate. The faith of the Eastern peoples has raised these kremlins in the name of Christ, and the setting sun wraps them in a fire more radiant than the kremlin of Moscow. Splendid color bathes the mountain and its cluster of religious buildings. As if to view the picture better, the *Waldeck-Rousseau* draws away; it moves between the sun, hung in a glory of rose-color, and Mount Athos, shimmering under the caress of the light. With its cliffs shining and its ravines filled with colors, it seems alive, and changes like a poignant harmony of violins. Into the summit, the frosts of December have driven a nail of snow, which catches the changing smiles of the sun and reflects them, soft and tender, into space. In a few moments the violet color takes possession of the sky; then it fades imperceptibly, and the *Waldeck-Rousseau*, for this night of the voyage, sails on in a religious atmosphere.

That man is to be pitied who is not moved by the enchantment of Nature, or who does not know the great lessons of history. He is ignorant of those pleasures that never fade. For fifteen days the Ionian Sea has been surrendering to me its secret of our inheritance from the Greeks. Mount Athos and this fair evening reveal to me another heritage, that bequeathed by Jesus Christ.

Long ago from the deserts of Palestine a voice was lifted among the Roman multitude. It brought back to earth those transcendant archangels whom the children of Cain had banished. The archangels are named Goodness and Justice. I will not pursue the story of their martyrdom here on earth. Like harmless little animals at bay before ferocious beasts, they have suffered; their hearts and bodies have bled; and the wicked boast that they have driven them from the world.

But a nation was found to receive these two trembling angels in her maternal hands. She revived them in her bosom; from their lovely touch she got the courage to suffer, and as the first Christians threw themselves to the torture rather than deny the Divine Master, so France for more than a century, has been willing to die in behalf of her love for Liberty and Justice.

In the month of August, 1914, with sword on high and bosom bare, she defied anew the perpetrators of cruelty. Her people and her ministers were not mistaken. Whether unbelievers or religious men, their gospel and their justification are those of the Galilean. It is indeed from His divine parables, and not from the decrees of the old Germanic god, that France has gathered the flower which is planted in her crest. White and incorruptible, this flower has closed its petals during the weeks through which we are living; but the German foulness shall not soil it, the shells shall not cut its stem, and the dawn is not distant when its opened petals will shed over the world a sweet fragrance.

How beautiful France seems to me, and how much in love with her I feel to-night! Frenchmen, realize your good fortune to have been nourished by so charming a mother! In the womb of antiquity were formed two priceless treasures: Greek beauty and Christian virtue. It is our France who has saved them from death. No people, no territory, has been willing to receive these heritages. Will all our blood suffice to pay for this unhoped for splendor? Take care lest we weaken. Under my eyes in the moonlight there glide past ancient lands and islands, my memories cross the centuries, rest like arches upon the supports of these legends, and form a bridge which leads far away to Jerusalem and to Athens.

Jerusalem and Athens! The barbarous Turks and the ignorant Romans have stripped the gilt from their glory. The sons of these two cities did not know how to defend their patrimony, and two thousand years of servitude, ruin and death, have delivered their helpless peoples over to the pity of history. Let us take good care not to imitate them. Ignorant and barbarian, the Germanic hordes menace us with their claws. The gracious mind and exquisite body of France are receiving the same affront as did her ancient sisters. But in this case the same catastrophe will not follow the same weakness.

Let us forget the frivolous thought and discourse of our former days. Beauty must be strong, and one can only smile when the fist is heavy. Let us suffer; let us know how to wait. From her dying sons France demands the right to shine resplendent. How much shall we not love her at the moment when, holding her spear, she undoes her iron tunic, and offering to the world a countenance flushed with feeling and eyes profound with the agony of battle, says in a voice broken with emotion and a smile brimming with pride: "I have consented to shed blood! Let me henceforth sow flowers!"

15 December, after the bombardment of British harbors by German cruisers.

We too could acquire this glory of slaughtering women and children. Who prevents us in the Adriatic? To-morrow, if the French sailors were bandits, the world would learn that their guns had bombarded unfortified towns and the Dalmatian Islands, and, protected by our cruisers' strength, had eluded the vigilance of Austria.

Where on earth did the Germans learn warfare! Does naval honor no longer exist among them? I cannot believe it. There are tasks which a sailor only accomplishes with rage in his heart, and those who fired at Yarmouth, Grimsby and Scarborough would ask pardon of God for the crime which their Emperor commanded. Only this man could have persuaded sailors to destroy peaceful towns. The sound of those shells he sent against a defenseless coast will whistle through history round his accursed name.

You, commandant of the *Emden*, Admiral of the cruisers sunk in the Falklands, captain of the armed liners, I can imagine you shuddering in disgust. Far away from the orders of your master, you caused a spotless standard to be feared on remote seas. Your conscience followed nobly the rules of war. You conquered. You have been conquered. In the great naval fraternity, no one thinks of uttering your names without taking off his hat to you. Before your defeat I would have pressed your brave hands, happy to touch fingers which no crime had sullied. But these cruisers of the North Sea, reptiles which smell of putrefaction—let them be tracked like stinking beasts—let them be executed like apaches of the sea, let them even be assassinated, and all sailors of the world, neutrals as well as belligerents, will think their punishment too good for their crime.

PART III
IN THE IONIAN SEA

End of December, 1914.

IT is nearly two o'clock in the morning. Far to the south glides a line of phantoms. We left Malta nearly a week ago; our monotonous cruising has almost effaced the very memory. It is a bad night. The rain is pouring down. The wind whips into our eyes and onto our lips handfuls of stinging nettles. I am shivering with cold. I see the file of boats and masts tossed by the swell. A British convoy is passing yonder, carrying Hindu regiments from the sparkling seas of Asia to the mists of Flanders. Its lights appear and disappear as it pitches on the water, and it does not notice our dark presence.

Although unknown as their guardians, the cruisers have made the seas secure for these transports, which could not resist the smallest enemy torpedo. At a distance the French ships accompany them, keeping between them and Austria, and at the end of the regular course, give over to other ships the duty of safeguarding them, and move away to new tasks. The boats that come from India and Australia might fancy the sea was empty and that good fortune was directing them to port. On certain clearer days, when they see almost imperceptible clouds of smoke, do they guess that these come from one of their guardian angels?

If our task consisted only in freeing the route for these exotic allies of ours, there would be reward enough for the difficulty of our labor. For the first time in the history of men, a war summons to Europe the children of immemorial Asia as defenders and not as devastators. Let us be the good artisans of this miracle.

Perhaps later, in some unforeseen voyage, I shall pass through some bazaar on the banks of the Ganges, or admire under the limpid sky the mystic lines of a temple of Brahma. With his head in a turban and his feet bare, a brown man will approach me, his eyes will laugh with pleasure at sight of a Frenchman lost among the Hindu multitudes. His white teeth will light up his smile, and he will murmur a few words of the language which is so beautiful it makes one tremble under every latitude:

"You, Frenchman! Paris.... Marseilles.... Good-day, monsieur!" this man will try to say. I shall turn back and return his smile.

"Welcome!" I shall answer, "to one who greets me in such pleasant words."

And we shall walk together. This man, born in the Punjab, the Himalayas or the Deccan, will draw a marvelous fresco from the treasure of his memories.

He will tell me of the battle of the Marne, the Oise or the Escaut. His eyes will have a profound, fixed look from having traveled in so many strange lands; his surprising metaphors will make live again the cities he saw during the intoxication of battle: Paris, Rheims, Ypres, and so many others. At certain moments he will take my arm, with respect at first, and then with confidence, as the ghosts of the past disengage themselves from a memory made drowsy by the Eastern sun. All the epic drama of Europe, already pale and unreal in his mind, will revive for the benefit of my melancholy joy.

Perhaps too, if God is willing, my friend of the moment will prove to have pushed his victorious adventure as far as Berlin. He will draw from his bosom a picture wrapped in rags, a post card showing Unter den Linden or the Brandenburger Allee. Under the blazing sun of India I shall contemplate dreamily these grim buildings, and my thoughts will make my heart beat heavily, though I shall not betray my emotion.

"You see, monsieur, I got as far as that."

He will put his finger on the Palace of the Kaiser, and the dignity of men who have accomplished great deeds will shine on his dark face. Silently we shall gaze at each other, living a unique moment together. And then something will break the charm, a street cry, a brawl of sepoys, or the barking of dogs. The Hindu will quickly hide the dirty picture, and will whisper more quickly still: "Afterwards I came back, and it was all over...."

We will go on a few steps, but he will remain silent, having finished telling me all the romance of his life. This romance will not return. No Hindu will live it again. Head down and hands folded behind my back, I shall find no words adequate to this dream of his, or to the shattering echo of our memories. On turning an alley, I shall offer him my hand, which he will doubtless kiss, and a few seconds later the eddies of the crowd will have parted us forever.

Go, charming Hindu with your sunny soul, towards the dream which enchants your slumber as you are cradled in the rolling of the transport. My lids burn and I am chilled to the marrow, but you have nothing to fear. The cruisers watch over your voyage and that of your brothers, for you are sailing towards France; and carry her your hearts and your arms, which are your only riches.

1 January, 1915; three o'clock in the morning.

I come down from the watch. My boots, my jacket, and my oilskins, drip in little dirty streams on the linoleum; my hair is matted with salt, and a bad headache, driven into my temples by the rain and the squalls, prevents my getting to sleep. The close cabin, hardly longer than a railway compartment, smells of rubber, of tar and is rancid. The steam heater adds a mustiness of hot metal; the exhalations of boilers and engines filter through the decks, and saturate everything with a stale odor; the hull receives the eternal blows of the sea's battering-ram that storms angrily against it. Through the joints of the port hole, which is screwed down as tight as possible, ooze threads of water which dribble along the wall and form a pool. For I know not how many days, the cabin has not received the least whiff of pure air, and the electric lamp shines grotesquely in the thick atmosphere.

With a towel, already soiled with coaldust, I remove the crust of salt and soot that is stuck on my face; then I wash my numb fingers in the little pool that dances at the bottom of my basin. Seated before my papers, my archives, I follow the movements of the cruiser as it rides the squall. Familiar lice and roaches risk timid voyages across my desk. A bold gray rat gnaws old cigar stumps and string in my waste paper basket. He is not afraid of me, and I do not disturb his little feast. What a sinister opening to the coming year!

Where was I just now, on the bridge enveloped in water? In the interval of my watch the year 1914 joined the dead and 1915 lived his first moments. A shower of rain gave its blessing to this agony and this birth, and a gale with lungs of steel howled with all its might. The clouds and the sea made a chaos in which sailors had difficulty in seeing anything, and the cruiser, tossed in the hollow of the waves, could scarcely keep its course. A hundred or two hundred miles away, other ships were burying their prows in this cataclysm of water, and struggling in the vast desolation.

The "naval army" is grieving over two recent disasters—the torpedoing of the battleship *Jean Bart*, and the loss of the submarine *Curie*. In the brotherhood of the sea, the injury or disappearance of a single ship creates a painful void.

The *Waldeck* did not take part in this last Adriatic expedition, in which the fleet went once more to tempt the Austrians. It had other tasks; without it, the cruisers, battleships and destroyers went up the liquid avenue, and spent some time there. After a futile waiting they returned in triumphant march to the strait of Otranto. Slightly enervated by their unprofitable effort, they were perhaps less strict in their vigilance, and went slowly, disdainfully towards an enemy restive for combat. But Austria, who accepted no fight in the open, had despatched on their course her venomous beasts. Through the lens of his periscope the commander of the submarine at Cattaro saw the splendid array of battleships rising on the horizon. The proud, thickset, form of the *Jean Bart* led the fleet on the return as it had led them on the ascent; on the mast floated the flag of the Commander-in-Chief, and his officers sadly surveyed the empty sea. But the Austrian, crouched in the waves, trembled at the approach of his unhoped for prize; each one of the men enclosed in the flanks of the submarine was keyed to the combat.

Oh! the minutes that these sailors and their commander must have lived through! Must one not envy them the emotion of their discovery and of decisive action at last? Boldness and courage erase frontiers; one feels jealous of an enemy for the supreme beauty of a dangerous coup like this. With all his energy concentrated in his eyes and on his lips, the lieutenant of the Austrian vessel watched the powerful battleships coming towards him; he maneuvered in short zigzags, to right and left, higher and lower, like an artist. If he showed himself, he and his crew would meet instant death. All the noblest and purest faculties of the officer rose in him. When his calculations and his experience told him that the *Jean Bart* had reached the fatal place, he gave two orders, and two torpedoes, at a few seconds' interval, threaded their way through the waves towards the hull.

One passed harmlessly behind the *Jean Bart*, and disappeared. But the other exploded against her prow. The heavy sound warned the sailors that the sea was seeking a victim. Through the breach the water poured into the breast of the battleship, tore open and twisted the compartments, and did not stop until it reached a wall strong enough to resist the pressure. Like a stunned fighter, the *Jean Bart* lowered her forehead and sunk her brow in the water. She carried more than a thousand men, but not one showed fear. Before disaster could happen, all of them did their instant duty, and the ship survived. By good luck the torpedo had been fired two or three seconds too soon; otherwise it would have destroyed her. In a few months she again took her place among us.

The *Waldeck-Rousseau* has had her own risks. Several times she has been attacked by submarines, but doubtless her very familiarity with this danger has kept her from being struck. Her crew are happy over her having escaped the fate of the *Jean Bart*. But what has the future in store? Let us continue to do our duty; let us watch with even greater vigilance, and keep our good ship from the hospital or the grave.

Since this accident to the *Jean Bart* we scarcely venture on the Adriatic except for very definite purposes. The enemy submarines have demonstrated their presence, which could be denied so long as none of our ships, through good fortune or skill, had been actually hit. It is a habit of men's minds to depreciate the danger which does not touch them. After the admiral's ship had been struck, the zone of operations was moved to the south, in the Ionian Sea. The "beats" of the cruisers are longer, and the weather is frightful. This sea is a regular gathering-place for the winds. Coming from the four quarters of the horizon, the sons of Æolus meet here and riot. The end of the Adriatic and Albania breed a keen icy capricious north wind which descends at a great velocity, rushing out of the corridor formed by the banks, expanding suddenly in the open, and turning the waves upside down. By way of Epirus and Morea, the winds of the east and southeast come from Syria and Asia Minor, and raise the stormiest seas. Endless fogs are carried over by the fringes of the simoon, from the hot south and the sands of the Soudan and Libya. And the strong west wind, born in the Atlantic, blown over Gibraltar and Sicily, rushes up and throws gigantic waves against the wall of the Ionian Islands, thrusts them back, cuts them and joins them again in wild and formless masses on which we leap and roll as if intoxicated. We see nothing but the gray elements of rain and wind, mist and spray. The ships avoid these latitudes, where few of the commercial routes cross, and which our presence renders still more undesirable. It is a sort of desert place in the city of the sea. Sea birds accompany us no longer; they fly in the heart of the gales. A troubled void, a journey of the Wandering Jew, that is the present existence of the cruisers.

Just now on going to the watch, my comrade and I, in order to celebrate the New Year, took to the bridge a bottle of champagne, a poor cheap bottle of champagne, some renamed Saumur, for our ship does not possess any rare vintage. In the shelter of the navigation-house, five glasses had been placed on the map of the Ionian Sea; they covered Sicily, Apulia, Corfu, the Pelopennesus and Libya; the bottle occupied the sector of the *Waldeck-Rousseau*, and in the storm awaited the five officers on duty. A black and icy rain was falling. The chill bit into one's flesh. When we stretched out our hands we could not see the tips of our fingers. A dripping steersman came howling in our ears—"Captain, it is midnight!" "Lieutenant, it is midnight!"

Bracing ourselves against a gale which almost tore us from the deck, we wiped our weeping eyes. We could not all get into the shelter-house; a group of two or three slipped in by turn and those who were not drinking continued the lookout. We stood under the wan streak of an electric light among books, confidential documents, maps, not daring to stir for fear of wetting these precious papers. We uncorked the bottle, which in popping made a pretense of sparkling, like our own false gayety. We raised the glasses. Drops of water fell from our sleeves and our fingers shook. We awaited the toast, but not one found anything to say. France invaded.... War stretching into the long future.... Our families, so far away.... So much sorrow.... No professional pleasures, and no hope of battle.... Accursed weather and a frozen body.... In our eyes shone something moist which was not rain; we were sad but tried to smile. The glasses trembled.

"To France!" I murmured at length. It was the only brilliant thing to come to my mind. "To France!" responded the others, and the glasses chattered against our teeth. No one finished his glass. After one swallow we could drink no more, but set our glasses down anywhere. The wind and rain rushed in by the half-open door, and one after the other, with choking hearts, we resumed our dim vigil on the bridge.

Two hours more before going below, two hours of tempest and anxious revery! Like a star shining in the midst of a hurricane, the mind watches in a body worn with fatigue. Across space the great tragedies of the dead year surge out of the past, and assemble in the mind of an officer harassed by the wind. Paris delicious in Spring and Summer.... Plans for the future.... The thunder of Serajevo.... The knife struck by Austria into the throat of Serbia.... The diplomatic storm.... The war.... The Prussians near Paris.... The immortal Marne.... The Adriatic hunts.... Drowning Russia.... Unchained Turkey.... Serbia invaded and freed.... Dramas of the sea.... Five months of exhausting cruises.... The submarine *Curie*....

3 January, after several watches and bad weather.

The *Curie*! Twenty days ago, I was talking with her Commander, who confided to me his hopes. A fine, intelligent-looking man, he thought with vigor and spoke gently. He was preparing a raid as far as Pola, an Austrian base, and gave me the technical details, and the arrangements for this remarkable enterprise. A reflective enthusiasm brightened his talk. Such an officer on such a boat, with the crew he described, was justified in attempting the impossible. I envied his good fortune.

But Fate, the god of sailors, did not wish him to win. Wireless messages informed us that the barrages had stopped the *Curie* in the very harbor of Pola. Later the survivors of this epic adventure will give the details of their audacity and their failure. To-day they languish in some Austrian fortress. God grant that some day I may press the hand of the Commander.

All alone, like the lost child of the "naval army," the *Curie* had started through the dangerous fields of the Adriatic. I do not know its route, the alarms it had, the ruses it used. Moving by night, hiding by day, darting its keen eyes over the horizon, it went along the coast of Italy as far as the Austrian line. At the end of the Adriatic it moved among ambushes; every wave of the enemy sea represented its winding-sheet. With body and soul equally hardened, the twenty-five men approached the hostile labyrinth. Their joyous hearts endured everything—the irregular meals, the suffocating atmosphere of the steel prison, the smell of oil, the whiffs of hydrogen, the sulphurous and oily vapors which make the head heavy and turn the stomach, the alternations of glacial cold and torrid heat as they came to the surface or submerged, the alarms and the dangers, the marvelous hope of penetrating the strongholds where the Austrian battleships had locked themselves in with a triple lock, the fear of running aground on the threshold, and the tempest of thought that crosses the minds of gallant men at the moment of action.

6 January, 1915.

One day, at the end of their hunt for danger, they see vague shadows on the horizon. It is the Austrian coast; it is Pola. Faint streaks of smoke hover over the further end of the well-guarded harbor where the Commander imagines the fleet to be. The prow of the *Curie* turns towards this cemetery; for whether it is their own or their enemy's; someone has to die in this adventure. Officers and sailors make the great dedication together, a generous offering of their youth and strength to their remote native land. The submarine submerges. They hear nothing more except the lapping of the waves on the ship, the purrings of the motors, as submissive as the obedient souls of the men, and the brief orders of the officer.

He and the others see nothing. But through the periscope the land rises into view, the smoke becomes black, the coasts reveal lighthouses, forts, promontories, and at last he perceives motionless masts. Between him and these masts lies the network of dikes, barrages and nets; against him the Austrian Argus levels a hundred eyes and a hundred arms—torpedoes, mines, guns, outguards, semaphores, and sentries. None of the sailors hesitates. Motionless before their valves and their hand-levers, they await the order of the man who is watching, and long to anticipate his will so that they can accomplish their task still sooner. They maintain the profound silence which precedes great deeds, and hope thrills in their hearts.

The steering-gear is handled, the manometers announce the various depths; the submarine touches bottom, and runs afoul on the shoals bristling with traps. An even profounder silence settles on all. Like statues of flesh, the men's hands are firm and their gleaming eyes are fixed on the man whose eyes in turn remain rivetted to the periscope. But one can guess from the quivering of his forehead, and the sound of his voice, the danger that approaches, the danger they are touching, the danger they are passing. "After God, the master on his ship!" says the naval proverb. This officer is a god, whose exactness of word and vision is responsible for the lives of twenty-five men; through the magic of confidence, they experience all his emotions.

The *Curie* has passed through. Obstacle after obstacle has been overcome. Through the increasingly bold behavior of their commander the sailors guess that the prize is near. Sleeping at their anchorage a short distance away, float the battleships. Who would have thought that a submarine, coming from the Ionian Sea, would ever penetrate into the very heart of Pola? The Austrian crews are off their guard; their officers, glass in hand, are doubtless stooping over the maps, and joking about the French Navy. It is a feast day. Whoever is not on duty is amusing himself on land. In the gay town toasts must be going round to celebrate the German victories, and in the squares the bands are playing Wagner or Brahms. Pola resembles some pretty town of Gascony or Provence, that is well protected from the enemy; between the morning paper and the evening communiqué she forgets the great drama of the distant war. But the *Curie* is moving about in the depths of the roadstead.

From this moment, the wireless messages tell us nothing; Austria acknowledges nothing. What did our submarine do? Did she disable, did she sink some ship that thought herself invincible? Or else, tacking towards the battleships, was she caught too soon in some treacherous barrage? The last news told of her being stopped by the steel meshes. Going or coming? The mystery will be well guarded. What despair, what death in the midst of life, when the twenty-five heroes of the *Curie* understood that they could get no further! They heard a grating along the hull; it was the prow penetrating the mesh, like a fish in the dragnet. Warned by this sinister sound, the Commander tried to reverse the engine, but the steering-gear at the side, with projections like fins and gills, was already entangled in the metal gauze. Then, however the *Curie* moved, the mass of the net softly followed, bending without breaking or permitting passage. How many times did her Commander repeat his maneuvers in search of safety? I do not know. What miracles of ingenuity did he not employ? I do not know. Every effort useless, he turned away his eyes, big with horror, from the periscope to the interior of the boat, and looked at his alert men, the great engine which he had directed to the goal and which would never return; he thought "We are lost!"

Did he pronounce these words? What if he did not! Everyone understood them and forgave. Since they had come either to die or to conquer, they accepted death along with the officer, and did not reproach him. They looked at each other with eyes that were melancholy but not afraid. They were merely regretful. They were ready for asphyxiation, poisoning, hunger, thirst, drowning, madness; all that was as nothing to the price of their failure.

While this was going on, electric bells in contact with the barrage, announced that something had been caught in it. The lookouts exchanged stupid glances, refusing to believe that it was a submarine. At first they supposed that a snag was moving the barrage, and were convinced only when they saw the eddies, and the bubbles of air on the surface which showed that a live thing was struggling below.

The hypothesis of a French submarine never occurred to them at all, and they telephoned the Admiralty, which became anxious. Some submarine of the station, returning to the fold, was struggling in the barrage, the intricacies of which it should have known. At once the chiefs summoned all the officers of the submarines, prepared to give a sharp reprimand to the foolish commander who failed to respond, after they had rescued him. But the officers all presented themselves. At length they all admitted that, in spite of the improbability, the devilish Frenchmen had reached the end of the channel. The admirals were silent, as one is silent before a miracle.

How many hours did the *Curie* spend in trying to break its bonds, like a noble stag stamping its hoofs and tearing its legs? But they could be saved neither by their knowledge, nor their prudence, nor their perfect audacity. No other crew, I swear, would have succeeded where they were stranded. Exhausted, the steel fish slowly rose to the surface.

8 January.

And the lookers-on saw the boat that had come from France. It was immediately showered with shells from guns and mitrailleuses, but the sailors, nearly asphyxiated, opened the narrow panels. Now that their death was no longer necessary, they consented to live, and the volleys spared this superhuman body of men who were surrendering. Pola assembled to see the landing of the sailors who had emerged from so impossible a feat. The survivors passed along, still staggering from their extraordinary adventure. I wager that the crowd made not a single unfriendly gesture against these martyrs. Perhaps, before these faces, so handsome and so terrible, and these ragged garments, the women crossed themselves, and the men saluted. The sailors of the *Curie* did not then receive the benediction of France, but in the respect of their conquerors they read the magnificence of their unsuccessful enterprise.

And we who sail the Ionian Sea award this crew the palm with invisible leaves. When in the middle of the storm, our imaginations begin to reconstruct this epic drama of our brothers, we envy them, we begrudge them the feat, and would exchange all the vagabondage still before us for the few hours which those men lived.

The admiration is not unjustified. In these days our enthusiasm is not spent foolishly. For the citations and the orders of the day create a roll of gallant men before whom one prostrates oneself almost as before angels. Before the war the most hopeful of us scarcely suspected that our wonderful race would prove so courageous. If we are so astonished and delighted, the world will be too. We live in an age which the Greeks would have peopled with demigods, and a Homer who attempted their celebration would scarcely have found words adequate to hymn them.

The fecund soil of France has given birth to all the virtues. There each soul becomes a tree on which flowers have suddenly grown. The coward becomes bold; the egoist, generous; the atheist kneels before his country. I fear that these miracles are not so evident to Frenchmen living on their native soil, but the exiled sailors are not deceived. And yet all they have to go by is papers and letters, black print upon white. Across these lines passes a breath like the pure wind which sweeps a dark sky. All becomes clear and bright. Perhaps one must be far away to admire the halo, shining fairer hour by hour, which encircles the destinies of one's country. The faults and errors vanish like dark spots on the gorgeous disk of the sun. Every French thought is a ray from a rising star. These rays are so warm, and carry so far, that they reach even us who live among the storms.

Day before yesterday I read two letters from the same mail. The weather was like the end of the world. Formless and gray, the mists poured over the troubled sea; the cruiser struggled in a circle of specters with liquid hair, who smothered the dying light. The two envelopes lay on my desk, that rolled as the ship tossed. In ink upon expensive paper, the first one contained an address in angular handwriting; the second was on cheap paper, in which the wavering writing had made holes. One gave forth a delicate perfume, which reminded me of the fair Parisian who alternated between love for her Pomeranian and the pretentious inanities of tango teas. To her husband, an encumbering sort of toy, she accorded only what the Civil Code ordered in the way of marital duties. The second envelope had no perfume; perfumed paper is unknown to the puny little stenographer whose services I made use of in Paris. She was a fierce anti-militarist; her father and her brothers talked themselves hoarse in meetings at the Salle Wagram, and I was often shocked at her anarchistic ideas.

In the first excitement at the end of July, it happened that I saw both women on the same day.

"You will see," said the first woman, resting a careless hand on my shoulder, during the tango "you will see that the common people will sabotage the mobilization. These fellows are rebels. Sooner than fight they will surrender to William."

To one of my subsequent questions she replied haughtily:

"My husband? My husband? What are you talking about? All the same they will not have the audacity to call out men of thirty-five!"

And, after a silence:

"I do not expect to lose him. We should go to the country."

The tango was finished without another word.

That same evening the stenographer brought me some pages. She was flushed, and her eyes flamed. I counted the pages carefully and paid her. Without looking, she pocketed the money, and remained standing, trembling. I was careful not to say a word.

"And you?" she said at last. "Would you go?"

"Certainly!"

"Well! It's your war!"

"My war?"

"Yes! The war of the upper classes, the officers, the idle people who carry swords!"

"Ah!"

"Certainly it is! You are going to make us kill ourselves to the last man, so that you can be masters afterwards."

"All the same, mademoiselle, you will keep your father and brothers. Their opinions compel them...."

"Hey? What's that you say?" interrupted the mutineer. "They have ordered their new boots, and papa refuses to guard the railroad. He wants to go to the front. But it is not for you they fight, ladies and gentlemen, but for France!"

God forgive me, I found nothing to reply. A few minutes later, having descended several steps, she became timid and correct, and leaned against the banister.

"You are going far away, sir.... The sea is terrible!"

"It is my profession."

"One can be drowned."

"One can swim."

"Would you be happy? Should you like it? Anyway, forget what I said. Can one write to naval officers?"

"They may even answer."

"Indeed?"

"Yes."

Her sharp heels rang on the staircase. And every month since she has written two pages to her patron, the officer, the bourgeois.

"My father is happy," says the letter in the last mail. "They have put him fifty kilometers nearer the Boches. My young brother has had his foot frozen, the other has lost his left arm, and won the *Croix de Guerre*. You see that all my people are well. They are bored in the trenches. They would like very much to get at the Germans. The officers say that that will come later. One believes them, doesn't one, because they get themselves killed first, and do not risk their men's lives? You are very fortunate to be an officer, and if in the navy they are like what they are in the army, I am well content with France which...."

Thus writes my rebel of former days; sincere to-day as then, she is the happier now for hating nobody.

"My dear husband," says the perfumed letter, "received a splinter of shell in his right shoulder. In fifteen days he can return to the front. I am obliged to feed him, for he has difficulty in using his other hand; he lets things drop into his beard, which is not nice. I should like to keep him, but I do not dare tell him so. I am not a heroic woman, and I am not afraid to acknowledge the fact to you. However, when I see these poor little soldiers in my hospital, who smile so sweetly in spite of their suffering, I understand that I have no right to keep my husband. If you could see these dear wounded men! They thank you so bashfully. They find simple words to express great things, and they look at their nurses with such kind eyes, and so respectfully that I feel unworthy to dress their wounds...."

Thus my idle lady. I am sure she has quite forgotten her old bitterness. I do not care to remind her of it.

All the letters that come from France are just as good, and contain sentiments that do not surprise me in the least. Wives, mothers and sisters of fighting men, have learned the sorrow of separations that may be eternal. Since my entrance into the Navy, how many such letters have I not received, each line betraying anxiety? But they were written by women of the sea, if I may so put it, women accustomed to anxiety. The majority of Frenchwomen were not acquainted with this style; but it did not take long for them to discover it. For the same anguish creates the same words.

These women hate war in the same way that our women curse the sea; they as much desire to keep their dear ones out of the terrible battle as ours rejoice when they learn that we were far away from a certain wreck or explosion. Their hearts are tortured by that suspense which makes them blanch at a telegram, and catch their breath at the sound of the postman's step. Who better than we naval men can understand the silent tears which will be shed by all the beautiful eyes of France?

By some secret sympathy the wives of soldiers use the same words which used to make us dream. They drive back their tears and try to smile; their letters tell us news, slip in anecdotes, and are silent about the mysterious scourge of the war. They carry themselves bravely, but the tones of their voices betray them. Near the beloved one, sharing his danger, facing the same death, they would be indifferent and cheerful. But they are alone. They can only wring their hands and raise them to God.

In times of peace only sailors were blessed with the love of these Penelopes, these Hecubas, these despairing Antigones; to-day this love is lavished on all the heroes of France. If they die in battle, the mourning in their homes will be like the mourning in so many sailors' homes: a dumb distress, faces buried in hands, bodies shaken by ceaseless sobbing. If they return they will see what our eyes have seen on our homecomings—these faces made sublime by the patient waiting, these eyes grown larger, these lips closed tightly on inexpressible suffering. They will know the long embraces, in which arms are stiff as chains of tenderness, and the mad beating of hearts, broken by infinite joy; they will listen to words that are never heard by those who never go away. Survivors, you will some day become acquainted with the poignant sweetness of the homecomings of cruisers, for to-day all the women of France are the wives of sailors.

Henceforth you will appreciate the power of simple souvenirs. A lock of hair, an amateur photograph, a muslin handkerchief, a penny pencil tooth-marked by some economical housewife—everything becomes a souvenir, everything creates homesickness. During long hours in the trenches or on sentry duty, these little objects will take you back to the sanctuary of your loves; you will appreciate the bonds of affection, to which perhaps you were careless because habit had disguised their sweetness. In the muddy furrow where your body is growing mouldy, and your blood is freezing, these secret amulets will warm your heart.

We too in our moving cabins keep priceless treasures and talismans.

10 January.

On this damp steel vessel of ours, where sometimes we are burning, sometimes frozen, the weather and the salt air discolor and thin out our memories. The faces that enchanted our lives take on smiles that are a little faded, watch over our weariness and our uncomfortable slumbers, and hold with us silent conversations, in which more is said than ever was said in other days. One's heart softens, one forgives, one makes new resolutions. The defects of the loved one disappear under new charm, and the proudest among us reproaches himself for ever having been rebellious.

After such conversations, the exile of the seas pursues his monotonous task with a lighter heart. The furnace of the engine-room and the icy bridge are thronged with phantoms who alleviate our austere labor with their invisible caresses. As at the beginning of the war, I should like to present a few pictures of the essentials of our existence, in which we kill time in tedious activity. But I can no longer do it. Nothing comes to me. The résumés in which I sum up our daily activities and which I extract from the log, are pretty significant. They are somewhat like the movements of a cloud, supposing it could think—its goings and comings, its risings and descendings, without ever being able to imagine either the causes or the effects. Why should I not merely copy here the journal of several days taken at random? The date matters little; the explanations which I shall add will apply just as well to past weeks as to months in the future.

SUNDAY. Sailed to a rendezvous in the bay of Katakolo where the fleet of battleships is stationed. 4.50 P.M.: anchored at Quilles S 77 E of the light of Katakolo. 6.05 P.M.: got under weigh in line behind the *Courbet*; the *Renan* and the *Democratie* behind us. The two other squadrons to the south. Night cruise.

MONDAY. 5.30 A.M.: in sight of the light of Katakolo. 3 A.M.: anchored at 1m.5 S 89 E from this light. Boats in the roadstead: *Courbet, Renan, Diderot, Danton, Condorcet, Mirabeau, Voltaire, Paris, France, Patrie, Democratie, Republique, Justice, Commandant-Bory, Chasseur, Voltigeur, Lansquenet, Canada*. 4.45 P.M.: weighed with the *Renan*. 6.30 P.M.: started on a route to south and west of Zante. Night cruise.

It was one of those Sundays in the Navy when everything is covered with gloom; weeping clouds, high seas, whirling icy wind. We were sailing steadily over a forsaken part of the sea, when a wireless from the Commander-in-Chief ordered us to the west coast of the Morea, to the bay of Katakolo. The dripping officers looked up the description and maps of this harbor we had never visited. As what we had to call evening fell, we approached the rendezvous. We could see nothing there. The rain came down in torrents, shutting out the view and almost the air and space. Suddenly there appeared the vague outlines of the ships, as if drawn in pencil and brushed over with glue. So short-sighted were we that we went near to them to be sure that these huge shapes were not tricks of the rain. Cowering in the rain, they seemed deserted, and we passed carefully between their motionless lines, as during a thunderstorm a traveler makes for his home through streets that are lined with houses set close together.

15 January.

Our anchor fell, and we heard nothing but the pattering of drops on the metal. As the night deepened our ship and our neighbors seemed to thin out like ink in a wash-basin; but the signals flashed on the mast of the *Courbet*, the Admiral's ship. Red and white, they had difficulty in crossing the rainy whirlwind, and their sparks made even more sinister this winter twilight. They ordered the squadrons to get under weigh. During the night, which is favorable to surprise attacks, the ships never stay in strange or open roadsteads.

All together we weighed anchor, and took our distances and our proper intervals. The night had completely fallen, the storm was increasing in violence, the unlighted ships groped about like blind men seeking their places in a ballet. Immense outlines approached, passed, disappeared, in the evolutions of the night; an error in the distance or route, a mistake in calculating the phantoms which moved all together, might have caused an irreparable disaster. At these movements nothing but their work exists in the minds of the sailors; family, country, war and affection, are abolished; one is simply a part of his vessel, like a gun or a smokestack.

While certain battleships, separating into two groups, sail to the south as a reserve, the *Courbet*, the *Waldeck*, the *Renan* and the *Democratie*, go in Indian file on the parallel assigned to them. One behind the other at a distance of a thousand meters, pitching and rolling for two hours westward, then two hours eastward, all night long they struggle through the waves. Through the stormy night the officers of the watch, in their turn, attend to their professional duties. Sometimes they lose sight of the shadow that is the ship ahead of them, and fear they are not taking the prescribed speed; they increase it, leaping ahead into the blackness; the rain redoubles, and they increase it again so as not to lose touch with their neighbor; the rain lessens, and an enormous mass, looming on the water, high in the air, rises almost within touching distance.

It is the ship in front, which the clearing of the rain suddenly reveals, and which we should ram if we did not reverse with all possible haste. Orders are sent to the engines, which slow down. The dangerous mass buries itself in the rain; the officer on watch is glad, and thinks: "All right this time...." At this moment, to his right or left, there emerges from behind a dark spot which does not at all resemble the rain. The officer observes it carefully. His inflamed eyes finally make out that the ship at the rear, which also has lost us, has increased its speed, and is about to ram us as we had just escaped ramming the other. He puts on speed; the ship aft diminishes, recedes, disappears in the darkness to fall back doubtless in a few minutes on the fourth ship of the line, which will have thought herself lost too, and been about to seek her comrades in her turn.

In the deviltries of this bad weather the officer in charge wears himself out solving these problems. Every minute of his watch is accompanied by a crisis, a pang, a cold sweat. His eyes meet only the gale, the stabbing gusts of rain, and downfalls of water. The hours pass. His eyes become painful burning circles. When he tries to sleep on his restless bunk, his eyes resist sleep, a sort of nightmare, accompanied by the rolling of the ship, makes illusory forms plunge before him in the darkness.

18 January.

In the morning the three groups of ships returned to the bay of Katakolo. This morning we found delicious, because the sun, though invisible, had whitened the edges of the clouds, and the monotonous rain had given place to brief showers; fragments of rainbow, scattered over the network of the waves, brightened the gray web of the sea. And land was near, fair, almost gay, under the false smiles of day, after being lashed by so many weeks of rain. At the edge of a little jetty some slender masts were swaying like bushes; from the white houses of the port a road emerged, winding among the rocks, the olive orchards, and the herds, towards a town situated on a hill. Green foliage covered the buildings of this little town, which the distance rendered imposing. Small imagination is necessary to give grandeur to the stones in Greek lands; as our eyes rested on these buildings, that were perhaps very ugly, they sought there some temple with classic colonnades or majestic portals. Illusion of our memory! This town is named Pyrgos, this province is Arcadia, and the brook which flows into the bay was formerly celebrated by the name of Alpheus; unconsciously we are paying its insignificance the homage which has been won for it by the divine liars of Greek poetry.

But why discuss such meager pleasures? This coast and anchorage are pleasant; would it not be more worth while to enjoy a few agreeable hours? Moreover, our order for departure has come, for it would be strange indeed for a cruiser to remain forever in one spot. The weather is spoiled, no more rainbows or showers. The rain begins to fall again, and shuts out all the light. The *Waldeck-Rousseau*, accompanied by the *Ernest Renan*, weighs anchor.

In a few minutes the two cruisers part from the battleships. When shall we see them again? They follow their vague courses in the south, wandering from roadstead to roadstead, and remaining in each without doing anything. They cover fewer miles than the cruisers, but their existence is perhaps duller. We watch, they wait; we run risks, they take shelter. Certainly I had dreamed of another kind of warfare, but I prefer the campaign of the cruiser to that of the battleship.

Just as troops in the army are transported by railway to the seat of operations, so the great ships tow the French submarines to the entrance of the Adriatic. Their base is in the bay of Plateali, behind the palisade of the Archipelago. Between two chases towards Pola and Cattaro, they assemble around an old battleship, the *Marceau*, which serves them as mother ship. The *Marceau* collects shipwrecked crews, renews the commissary, furnishes its tools for repairing the small engines. Anxious to get away, the sailors of the submarines work with file and anvil, and are happy when they shorten the delay by a day, or an hour.

We go to look for the *Gay-Lussac*, whose turn for refitting has arrived. After a night of heavy seas, the *Waldeck-Rousseau* clears the narrows of Dukato. In default of fine weather, she finds here a little calm. Ithaca, Cephalonia, Santa Maura, the Echinades, and the splendid mountains of Epirus are capped with mist; a foaming sea rages round their base; brooks cover them with a silver network. Some strips of fog float in the channels, cling to the rocks, and tear apart like carded wool.

A winding channel opens out on the cove of the submarines and the *Marceau*. Crouched in the depths of their den like a nest of strange animals, they look gray and shiny; a thread of smoke is rising lazily from the battleship; the *Gay-Lussac*, ready to depart, is throwing from its stacks short black wreaths of smoke. Islands and rocks form an enclosed frame all about the waiting *Waldeck-Rousseau*. Some rocks are formed like saws, crafty and dangerous reefs, scarcely emerging from the water; others suggest a face left unfinished, where some capricious giant, after sculpturing the rough outline of a chin, a nose, or a jaw, has fixed them there forever; certain ones reveal exquisite curves, which one wants to caress like the back of a supple cat or the thigh of a statue.

The *Gay-Lussac* detaches itself from the group, and emerges from Plateali. On our after deck a group of seamen are arranging the towing tackle; the prow of the submarine halts a few meters from us, and we make the proper maneuver. We can distinguish the features of our comrades in their cramped black garments. Their young faces, ruddy with a fine color that has been tanned by the spray, are gravely happy. A few words are shouted down to them; brief responses come back.

"Are you ready?"

"Quite ready."

"Do you need anything?"

"Nothing at all, thank you."

"We can start?"

"Go ahead!"

The steel cable unrolls in the water, measures its length, tightens, threshes about like a serpent fringed with foam, falls back, and the submarine begins to follow us. Cautiously we increase the speed to the prescribed rate, and begin the passage of the straits and channels. We cannot easily perform evolutions, because the *Gay-Lussac*, two hundred meters behind us, would ram us if we doubled too short.

The destroyer *Mousqueton* heads the procession, moving with ease and grace. All muscle and speed, her pretty body winds through the islands, the guardian angel of our present cruise.

Towards evening we come out on the high seas. The bad weather has not become permanent, but the crossing will be unpleasant because of the short choppy swell that comes from Corfu and Santa Maura. Already the *Mousqueton* is covered with showers of spray; the *Waldeck-Rousseau* slowly heaves and rolls; at the end of the towing-line, which vibrates like a rubber band, the *Gay-Lussac* bounces in the swell. The dull twilight comes on; the clouds descend a little lower, the wind rises, a gray night follows the slaty evening, and we begin the crossing which will be twelve or fourteen hours like so many others.

In the middle of the night I take the watch and look for my two comrades. If I did not know that they were there, I should have difficulty in finding them. An indistinct spot in front of the prow seems to keep us company; it is the *Mousqeton*. She rises and falls like a dripping black cloth which a laundress shakes incessantly. She lurches ceaselessly right and left, without finding any support, and reflects restless gleams in the night. Thanks to this dark artificial fire, I do not lose track of her.

The *Gay-Lussac* is following us back there among the hills of water. The sentries on our cruiser, on the side of the towing-line, can tell by touch whether it remains taut; as long as the cable is tight, the submarine has not left us; nothing except its sudden slackness could warn us of a break of the line. Several times I go down to the after deck, unable to tell with my eyes whether the *Gay-Lussac* is there or not, but the tension of the cable reassures me.

Towards dawn Fano rises on the horizon, and near six we prepare to cast off the submarine. Our engines slow down; we haul in the cable. The officers have interrupted their sleep, and Mgr. Bolo, always curious about the sights at sea, leans on the rail for the last maneuver. On the submarine the sailors, like shining tritons, loosen the tow; its commander raises his arm to indicate that he is free; his screws make an eddy in the water, he turns its head to the north, and the *Waldeck-Rousseau* turns to the west. The Albanian mountains watch over this silent parting. How small the submarine looks, swept by the ceaseless waves! How weak it seems as it goes to risk its life in the vast ambushes of the Adriatic! And how melancholy is this silent departure, without a handshake, in the rainy and sullen dawn! From the height of our great ship we feel our hearts tighten. It is much like seeing a little child cross alone a square where automobiles are passing, one wants to say: "Don't go any farther. Come back on the sidewalk." And at the same time one approves its boldness, and encourages it from the depths of one's heart, without even thinking of the danger. The sailors of the submarine no longer look at us. Their eyes scan the sea, at the end of which they are to fulfil their duty. One desire alone fills their souls; to play their part well and not to weaken. They are not angels. The life of each one of them undoubtedly contains many faults, and I would not swear, that when they are turned loose on shore, they do not give way to every intemperance. But at this moment those ugly things no longer exist. However gross in their failings, sailors are noble in their deeds. At the instant that the *Gay-Lussac* passes behind us, the officers raise their caps, and the priest, without a word, extends his right hand, blesses and absolves these gallant men.

They go back up the path which the *Curie* traversed. They go to hold the sentry-post of honor before the enemy coasts, and none can foretell their fate of glory or death. Like their brothers they seek in the Dalmatian Isles before Cattaro some ship worth sinking. But probably the Austrian spies have not failed to follow our cruise, and the *Gay-Lussac* will find nothing. For three or four days, to the limit of its breath and its electric power, it will prowl invisible. Through the lenses of the periscope its commander will see the aviators describing great circles in search of it; he will make out the onset of the destroyers, will hide himself in the depths of the sea, and will hear the passage of the screws above him, frantic but impotent.

20 January.

One evening, out of breath, aching in body and soul, he will descend the Adriatic, the Ionian Sea, the Archipelago, to the harbor where not even repose will be his reward. The entire "naval army" when it hears the news will breathe more lightly at the wireless which announces: "The *Gay-Lussac* is returned." And will share in its discomfiture at the postscript: "It has seen nothing." It will hardly have left the shores of Austria when the ships will begin to move more freely, until the coming of the next one. Such is the Odyssey of the submarines of Plateali. Good luck, *Gay-Lussac*!

22 January.

The *Waldeck-Rousseau* has left the Albanian waters and reached its cruising sector. The Ionian Sea is divided into rectangles of vast extent, each one of which represents the territory of a cruiser. There she patrols for several days, reaches the next sector, and so on until she comes near land. Then she coals in all possible haste, goes to the farthest rectangle and begins all over again. Our post for the day is far in the west near the strait of Messina, at the end of the Italian boot, and we do not reach it before twilight. We take a route outside the cruising zones.

Two masts and four smokestacks rise on the horizon like a play of shadows. It is the *Gambetta* prowling about. She sights us, approaches swiftly, assures herself that we are friends, turns back and disappears. For several hours we see nothing but the surge of water and the clouds of shifting slate. And then the *Michelet* looms up in her turn, having just recognized us. We profit by this proximity to perform a telemetric exercise. In the course of this exercise the two cruisers execute a hundred movements which bring them together, and separate them, by anywhere from five to fifteen thousand meters; the gunners at their places, the telemetrists at the measuring apparatus, at the proper moment note the distances. Ships which meet by chance do not fail to indulge in this practice. A signal rises to mark the end of the exercise.

The *Michelet* returns to its patrol, and we push towards the west. By evening a great wall bars our horizon. Later a light gleams out with a pale track across the water. The lighthouse is called Rizzutto, and shines at the base of the Calabrian mountains. If the weather were more favorable we could see the summit of Etna in a clear atmosphere. Its beautiful outline would make us forget the proud heights of Albania, in front of which, this morning, we parted from the *Gay-Lussac*. But the sailor must be satisfied with a gloomy evening and a sullen sea; his only friend at night will be the light of Rizzutto, which we shall lose and find again as we move towards the offing or towards the coast. We have another companion in the wind, which whistles itself out of breath, perhaps for fear we should think it asleep.

Early in the night, as the cruiser nears Calabria, a sort of luminous halo plays over the land. We recognize the aureole of a town. Over there, human beings are at rest, or amusing themselves, or talking pleasantly before sleeping. Here, dressed in leather and rubber, the sailors struggle with the gale and defy shadows in which danger may lurk. This contrast haunts the minds of the lookouts. Are they happy in their sentry duty in the rain? Do they envy the Italians sheltered in their peaceful homes? The two ideas alternate, and in order the better to curse the Calabrians who are giving them not so much as a thought, the sailors look for the name of this troublesome town on the map.

It is called Crotona. In the days when Rome was weak and Athens powerful, she waged repeated and bitter war against her rival Sybaris. Softened by too much luxury, the Sybarites could not defend themselves against their powerful enemies, and Crotona, after effacing her voluptuous enemy from the world, survived throughout the centuries to show the light of her lamps this night to some passing French sailors.

Have we not a right, we officers, companions of the darkness, guardians of a crew of gallant men—have we not the right to send our dreams across the war to the regions of antiquity? The carefree Sybarites left a name which serves only for jesting. The map is almost ignorant of the exact places where they ignominiously disappeared, and the pick of the excavator exhumes only chalky debris. The people of Crotona bequeathed the future to proud descendants, because the sweetness of life did not make them disdain war. A stern lesson which we repeat in the biting north wind and the rolling waves; a parallel which forces itself upon one in these hours when France gathers herself together against the barbarians. But I have no doubts about her. The men of the *Gay-Lussac* who went this morning towards Cattaro, the men of the *Curie*, who were stopped by the glorious net at Pola, the men of the "naval army" who since August have lived in company with hardship, the men who freeze in the trenches of Artois and the Vosges, the men who have fallen on the plains of Flanders and Champagne—these men will not play before posterity the rôle of Sybarites.

25 February.

Like feudal barons, who lance in hand ride over their empty manors ruined by war, the cruisers traverse a lifeless waste. During the slow succession of days, they are glad to sight, by chance, the stacks of their companions of the patrol. As she comes to the boundaries of her rectangle, the sister ship seems to give us a nod and a good-day. Suddenly our world is alive again. Our thoughts are directed toward our neighbor, and her's toward us. Whether it is the *Renan*, the *Quinet*, the *Gambetta*, or an entirely different one, we follow her and accompany her movements; the sailors abandon their work and their reveries for this reality which wavers before them.

"She is approaching!"

"I see her bridge!"

"Look, the forestack is pouring out black smoke. They are stoking up the fires!"

"Ah! She is coming on the left. Her masts are passing one after the other."

"Are we not a good twenty-two thousand meters away?"

"She is farther away. Do you still see her masts?"

"Yes! No! Yes! No! No more."

The cruiser vanishes and our world becomes empty again. This lasts a day or a week. Sometimes between two clearings of the weather some darker spot appears in the distance, cloud or mountain, cliff or play of the clearing storm, no one can say. But the mechanics and the stokers, the hidden hosts of the depths, who come on deck between two watches ask curiously in the darkness:

"What do we see over there?"

The gunners and seamen, with a grand manner, repeat the scraps of officers' talk they have overheard and remembered. They announce the oracle: "It is Epirus;" "it is Apulia;" "it is the Peloponnesus;" "it is Albania;" "it is Etna;" "it is nothing at all; we are a hundred miles from land." The baffled men store up these complicated names, and in the next letter to their fathers or to some women in the country, each will write them down painfully; the strange words will carry to French cottages the echo of our geographical Odyssey. I should like to know the impressions made by these sonorous names, full of dignity, but without meaning to the ignorant. What do our brave sailors see in this fresco of coasts which we never approach? They are like the imaginary forms created in sleep; wavering, rising, disappearing on the borders of the horizon, they pass like Edens where we shall never land. The cruiser goes and comes on its rectangle of water, and while the officers strive to guess the meaning of this formless nothingness that emerges from the rain, the sailors pursue their dreams, the rain falls or is blown away in the caprices of the gale.

Yes, we pay to the hilt the ransoms for our patrolling! Nothing moves on the sea any more that carries an enemy flag. Nothing suspect approaches us. Masters of the seas, we have made it a desert for those who do not work for our side. If I dared, I should say that we have done our task too well, for everything which our country gains through our vigilance, we lose in boredom. The days of visits and searches is over; even these small distractions have fled from our daily labors. If there are contrabandists, they stick like woodlice to neutral shores, and carry to Austria or Turkey, at the price of increasing risks, the precious goods which become rarer every day. Their detours are long and laborious, but we cannot harass them so long as they frequent the territorial waters. Sensitive to their sovereign rights, Greece and Italy, by the regulations of war, do not permit us to approach their coasts; we are condemned to remain in the offing which our persistent surveillance has devastated. Doubtless Austrian submarines are moving under the waves. The hour for one of us will perhaps strike. Woe to the ship that becomes careless through lassitude!

But at least, on the great routes from Gibraltar to Suez or Saloniki the English and French transports are sailing without impediment. Formerly their fleet moved westward carrying to Marseilles or the Atlantic ports the men and products of the East. But for several weeks, since the entry of the Turks into the war, a second route has been established and is more frequented every day. Bases of operations are being installed in the Ægean Sea, in the Greek Islands; naval forces are assembling there; a few detached cruisers watch the coasts of Syria and Asia Minor; and multitudes of active troops are congregating down there.

2 February.

All these movements go on in silence, the silence that is the proper preparation for enterprises of war. The world does not yet suspect what is going on; its ears have not heard those names which, unknown to-day, will before long become famous. But the sailors pursue the task, and their souls quiver with joyous anticipation of these military glories in the East.

Sometimes, from a cloud charged with lightning, there is slowly detached a massive shred, that one can scarcely distinguish as it glides upward to some clear portion of the sky. The cloud swells, extends and forms into a new storm which rages, far away from the clouds which engendered it. Thus, born from the European War, a new war is in secret ferment; before the thunderbolts fall on the lands of Islam, we are preparing them in the mysterious and silent seas. We are acquainted with the daily effort, the cautious approach of the Allies, the legions of gallant men who caress their guns during the long Mediterranean crossing. But we take no pride in this knowledge. We expect to go on protecting the march of the soldiers towards glory. And we hope for the supreme joy of sharing their risks, hand in hand, so to speak, they on land, and we on the restless element of the sea.

At present the seventh week of our pilgrimage is closing in hail and frost. Since our trip to Malta, before Christmas, we have experienced all the evil moods of the weather, which grows angrier and angrier. At night, one falls and hurts oneself on the sleet-covered steel decks, as on a hard mirror invisible and yet in motion.

5 February.

Like seed thrown by some terrible hand, the hailstones bounce on the cruiser, which rings like a tambourine; and the sea, whipped up by these projectiles from the sky, makes a noise like a boiling liquid. The organ of the winds harasses our watches. Dismal and raucous, they stride breathlessly over the miles of water; their rage vents itself on the ship, and on our bodies, in icy handfuls of spray; when they strike against the cordage and metallic structures, they whistle and sing like evil geniuses filled with mirth. We know the harmony of each cord, of each halyard, of each cable, as they vibrate above our heads. Whether short or long, thick or thin, made of hemp or twisted steel, they have their share in the tireless orchestra. Certain ones give out in the north wind a clear and joyous sound, like a fife, bagpipe or flute. Others, melancholy strains like cellos and oboes, reminding one of the bells of one's native village, of beloved distant voices, of all the sweetness of France to one forlorn in nights of exile. But the hollow, tolling notes that are thrown from the heavy, wet cordage, sound a perpetual knell that is heard above everything. If one stops one's ears, their sinister bass penetrates one's fingers and head. They are always there. They are triumphant. To the cold of the body they add the chill of the soul.

6 February.

Montenegro is dying of hunger. From the top of its barren mountains its people can see the Adriatic, and imagine the prosperous lands in the distance, Africa and Italy and their crops. Towards these bountiful harvests they stretch their appeals and their greedy hands; but famine, following war, is devastating their homes.

Despite her own agony, France does not suspect into what horrors the present tragedy can plunge the peoples who are cut off from the world. In Paris and in the provinces there is food, and subsistence. Whatever the price, meat and bread can be bought at the butcher's and baker's. Montenegro has nothing. Walled up in a dungeon, its women and its soldiers scatter to the four winds appeals which do not feed them.

From the north, Austria is waging against it that same campaign of devastation which she began against the Serbs. To the south, Albania, that courtesan of pillage; only waits the command to throw her bands into Cettinje. To the East, Serbia, hemmed in, remains alive only by a tenacity which will amaze the future. And, finally, towards the West, the sea, closed to the nations without navies, leaves deserted the harbors of Montenegro, and empties her granaries.

In spite of that, she does not hesitate. At the first insults hurled against her by her Slavic cousins, each man took his cartridges, wound around his legs the puttees of war, and went to the frontiers to fight in defense of honor. If I had not forbidden myself to inscribe here events which have nothing to do with the Navy, I should tell of this drama of skirmishes, raids, night assassinations, in which a handful of mountaineers, without arsenals or foundries or commissary supplies, or routes or guns, renews every week, against the immense armies of Austria, the exploits of Leonidas against Xerxes.

But this perseverance, invincible to the attacks of men, has to yield to the sufferings of the body. To conserve energy in his muscles, precision in his eyes, firmness in his will, the Montenegrin has to have food. They call for help. Since snow and mud have taken possession of their kingdom, Prince Nicholas and his ministers send out wireless messages of supplication. Smothering their invincible pride and the shame of yielding to hunger, they tell us every day the story of their distress. Just now, in some district that had been bombarded by heavy artillery, the storehouses were burned, and the meager provisions of a year destroyed. Another day, Croatians and Bosnians, pursued by the Austrian butchers, took refuge in ruined Montenegro; as gifts they brought only their hate and their hunger.

Nevertheless, this little agrarian population opened their arms, and for these people without a country they deprived themselves of a pinch of wheat from their own pittance. Our wireless poles receive a new story of distress every moment; the children are dying, the soldiers have no more shoes, the cartridge boxes are empty, and the mules are dying along the roads where they find nothing to eat but snow.

Who will feed these unfortunates unless it be generous France? For months the "naval army" has supplied Montenegro. In the Ionian Sea cargo-boats come to get orders from the Commander-in-Chief, and then go to the ports of Antivari or Medua. They bring wheat, corn, equipment, munitions, and empty them in haste on the wharves, fearful of these dangerous waters.

These are enterprises for contrabandists and pirates. The Austrians know our least movement, spy upon the arrival of our cargo-boat; and their submarines, and aviators, and destroyers, make any unloading by day impossible. Everything has to be done at night, between the setting and the rising of one sun.

Far from the coasts a squadron ascends the Adriatic. It is composed of a precious battleship, some destroyers and large cruisers. We keep a careful lookout, for the enemy lies in wait. At the fall of evening, the squadron arrives off port; the cargo-boat and the destroyers turn aside; the cruisers push farther north towards the approaches of Cattaro, in order to prevent the first attack. At a little distance from the roadstead where they unload, a line of destroyers cruises about all night, ready to repulse any sudden attacks. In the harbor itself are anchored one or two other destroyers, motionless sentinels of the affair. The cargo-boat approaches the wharf.

There is nothing to be seen. The rain, wind and hail fall in avalanches from the icy heights. We must not show a light. Montenegrin soldiers try to offer their assistance, but they know little about delicate maneuvering, and in the darkness they get in the way. Somehow or other the commander of the cargo-boat manages to get it alongside the wooden jetty; he strikes it, tears his hull, breaks the hawser, swears and storms. The sailors of the destroyers come to help; they find their way to the wharf in small boats. With agile fingers and feet they grip the uprights, take hold of the cables and gropingly make them fast. The boat clings tight to the quay, and immediately a stream of sacks, cases and bales pours out. The Montenegrin soldiers come up, seize the black things in the darkness, drag them up the bank, run, stumble, fall. One must work quickly and keep silent. Up above, the camps and the huts are waiting.

But a noise in the air makes us prick up our ears. It comes from the north, a droning which is louder than the wind. It grows, and intrudes itself into the darkness like a sonorous wail. Another sound, duller, from farther off, accompanies it and draws near. Others follow, like dark wasps. These are the aviators from Cattaro. The sound of their flight rolls in the air above the harbor, diminishes and descends, makes a circle about the wharf, diminishes and descends again, directly above the cargo-boat. The target is indicated by the heavy sound of the bales and the hurried steps. A shower of bombs falls.

It is impossible to respond. The Montenegrin coast is not organized against aviators. The projectors that one could light on board would only draw the shots with greater precision; the crews, handicapped, occupied with the unloading, cannot fire guns or cannon. On the wharf, in the water, on the deck of the boat, the bombs burst, setting fire to the woodwork and the cases, mixing with the storm a suffocating smoke. Terrified by this unaccustomed enemy, the Montenegrin soldiers grow slack; the sailors, however, pursue their perilous task humming a song.

Sometimes a shell falls into the hold which is being emptied. If it bursts, some men are mowed down; if it rests harmlessly on the piles of sacks, hands seek it in the dark, seize it, throw it into the water, and the work continues. Exhausted by past watches, the crews work through this night without losing a second, and find means to stow neatly the sacks which will be of no use to them. No matter which destroyers and cargo-boats take part, the same business goes on at the wharves of Antivari and Medua every three or four nights.

While this is going on, the destroyers maintain a defense at the opening of the bays. The hearts of the men are anxious when they hear the fall and see the bursting of the bombs over their toiling friends. But their own turn is not long delayed. Before returning to Cattaro the airmen do not hesitate to drop their visiting cards on the sentinel squadron. But for fear of betraying their position, the latter do not reply. At their post on the sea, wiping the spray from their faces, the sailors hear the descent of the bombs, screaming in the north wind, and keep their spirits equally high whether the shells touch or miss the mark.

8 February.

Further out, further north, the cruisers scout between Cattaro and the menaced harbors. Towards the end of one of their Ionian cruises, the Commander-in-Chief designates them in succession for this work; they do not care for these expeditions in which there are blows to receive, but none to give.

For from beginning to end of these voyages to succor Montenegro danger is present. Every time the cruisers ascend the Adriatic, they meet with mines set loose by the Austrians, which trail adrift, like evil beasts too lazy to run after their prey. On our last cruise the *Waldeck* and her comrade saw several, though the brown speck is scarcely distinguishable upon the blue carpet of the waves. We approached them at a respectful distance, for fear they might be bound together like beads, and that other mines, invisible, would hit us as we passed. We demolished them with gunfire, without halting; they burst and sank, throwing off an inoffensive sheaf of yellow smoke. But what will happen to the ship that strikes one of them in the thick of the darkness, where one sees nothing?

And then, as the cruisers do every time, we watched all night the approaches of Cattaro, ready to receive the submarines and destroyers which will not fail sooner or later to attack the supply-boats at Antivari or Medua. In the misty, rainy atmosphere the searchlights of the Austrian harbor flash and sweep the sea, searching for the enemy they suspect to be within range. These great white restless eyes wander ceaselessly to right and left, and halt sometimes upon us. But the cruisers are so far away, shrouded in rain, that the enemy confuses them with the sheets of rain that are falling. Behind their guns, lighted up like specters, our gunners hold themselves ready to reply to the fire of the batteries if they begin. But nothing happens except a silent waiting; the searchlights abandon our vague outline, and go on indefinitely sweeping space.

From hour to hour our anxious wireless asks news of the unloading. And the destroyer anchored near the cargo-boat answers in short phrases:

"Rain and hail. Half done."

Or else:

"Very bad weather. We do not expect to be through before six in the morning."

As night wears away, thanks to the tension of mind and the bad weather, disquietude increases on the cruisers. They would like to be nearer, sharing the danger of the others. They fear some catastrophe before dawn.

The other night we saw some suspicious lights in that direction; short sparks like will-o'-the-wisps which succeeded in traversing the leagues of rainy air. The officers on the watch stood by helpless at these signs of the drama that must be going on. Soon the wireless despatch arrived, and was feverishly translated by the ensign on duty.

"The airmen are bombarding us. The bombs are exploding on deck. One fell into the hold. All the Montenegrins have fled and taken shelter on the shore. We fear we shall not be able to finish at dawn. The Austrians continue the bombardment."

Immediately the *Waldeck* replied:

"If there is too much danger, or you are no longer numerous enough, stop the unloading, leave the harbor; we are coming to your assistance."

Without waiting for a response, we made for the bombarded harbor, moving at top speed, for fear we should arrive too late. But in less than ten minutes our rush was stopped short by the wireless reply, which showed their astonishment at our proposition.

"We will continue alone. We will not leave until daybreak. There is almost nothing left to unload."

They did as they said! They did even better. How did they find means to increase their strength, to make up for the flight of the Montenegrins? They did not even think they had done a big thing, but at dawn the holds were empty, and on the wharf were heaped to the last one the bales that had been in their charge. Ah! the brave sailors!

9 February.

Long hours flow away. The January nights seem eternal when one has to live them wide awake. But at last the sky pales in the East, the lights of Cattaro sink into the grayness and a sharper cold revives the watchers a little. It is dawn.

Empty or not, the cargo-boat casts off its hawsers, and as clumsily as it entered the night before, it leaves in the morning. On the wharf are heaped the supplies for Montenegro; more will be brought in a few days. The stevedores go back to the destroyers, and exchange their night's fatigue for that of the engines and the work of navigating the ship. The procession forms again in the mist, and goes down the coast of Albania in good shape. Without ballast, the cargo-boat dances in the midst of the convoys like a cork. At a great distance the cruisers continue their proud vigil until all this little company is out of harm's way. Then they feed their fires, stretch their legs, and limber up with a little gallop as far as their Ionian sectors.

Or else between sunrise and twilight, they coal in some hidden bay. And if chance favors them, they receive letters, and bundles of papers which have wandered in pursuit of them over the vast sea. Although it has left France so many weeks ago, and is already old, and made stale by events, the news is read and commented upon with passion.

The sailors are not turned aside from the great drama by any mediocre or banal concerns. Among all the people of the world, it is they who vibrate most strongly to all the joys and troubles of France. Their clear vision, free from passion, judges calmly the conflict of the two parties. Better than anyone, thanks to the patience of their pilgrimages, they discern in the future the reasons for victory and the heavy ordeal of attaining it.

Bent on their secret task, they do not heed the dazzlement of victories. They know that their collaboration, decisive as it is, will be effaced by the future prowess of the soldiers. The gunfire, the charges, the final drama for which the land will be the theater, will relegate their silent labor to oblivion. But to overthrow Germany both will be needed, and the glorious army can hold out a grateful hand to the Navy.

Already our fleets are closing the doors of the world upon our enemies, and keeping them wide open for the resources that will feed our victory. As yet it is nothing; but hour by hour we forge a new lock. When Germany and her allies, foaming with rage in the prison to which our ships are the bars, suffer the tortures of famine; when the one hundred and ten millions of Germans, howling at death's door, demand pity, and beg a bit of bread, when this menagerie tears itself to pieces in the struggle for food; when revolt, insurrection, and the frenzy of civil war shake to its foundations this manufactory of murder; then, Russia, England and France will let loose their bulldogs and their tamers. From their bridges the marines will hear the footsteps of the soldiers' charge and the barkings of their 75's. Their hearts will leap with joy, and, gazing at the sea, the companion of evil days and luminous sunrises, they will say to her: "It is we two together who have made it possible for all this to happen."

Why does my vision wander to those happy days, our recompense? Is it because of the contrasting melancholy of winter? Or else, have I not been conducted thither by a natural path, through the letters of comrades, the illustrious marine fusiliers in Belgium? Since their wounds have got better through hospital treatment and convalescence, they have commenced writing again. Nearly all my friends over there are dead. Those who remain describe in simple language the trip to Antwerp, the return in the horror of the conflict, the resistance so savage that our enemies will never acknowledge that it was this handful of brave men who blocked their rush. History will reward these officers, these sailor-soldiers whom we knew on the deck of the men-of-war. Where they have been, we should all like to have fought. The entire "naval army" is jealous of this naval brigade. Exiled from the sea, they were acquainted with the cyclones of the struggle. Separated from the hurricanes at sea, they did not lower their heads before the mysterious thunderstorms of the Yser and Flanders. They paid the price of their courage in a terrific hecatomb; the barrier where the German invasion was stopped is built on blue collars and red pompons.

We shall never see again those naive faces which laughed at the tempest. Their death was not such as they would have chosen; they have had to pass to their eternal rest beside the bank of a canal or a marsh, with their hands tightened on their guns and a last smile fluttering on their eyelids. When their brains reeled with the dizzy agony, and their torn limbs were trembling, they could imagine themselves in the grip of the sea's great surges, and glimpses of its vastness floated through their last visions. Under the gray skies of the Belgian plains, their glazed eyes saw the skies of typhoons; the mud in which they sank took for the moment the odor of their native spray; in delirium their ears recognized in the noise of the shells the blows of the waves on the hull; in the whistling of the balls the sound of the wind as it makes the cordage vibrate as if under violin-bows. All this drowns out the usual memories that accompany one's last hours—the chiming of village bells, the murmurs of a sweetheart or old grandmother. For there are two things in the world which a man never forgets—the fascination of the sea, and the tenderness of women. But when the soldier approaches the threshold of eternity, the phantoms of the latter disappear before the last appeal of the former.

All these things I read in the narrative of the survivors. They remember the lightning storm which preceded this emptiness from which they have come back. Unaccustomed to the march, they could not think of the sea during those atrocious days when at each step their feet and their knees became heavier with a weight that fairly nailed them to the ground. But they went on just the same. They did not think of the sea when their breaking lines recoiled before the German flood. Neither could they think of it under the storms of shells. But at the minute when they wavered between life and that which has no name, they all received the final kiss of the sea. Its whispers cradled them, and they were grieved that they could not be buried in its watery grave. Thinking of their comrades, they bequeathed to them the hope of perishing in its enveloping arms, during some heroic combat.

From their hospitals and homes the survivors send us their good wishes. Towards the East, towards the Dardanelles, the world is beginning to direct its attention, and the ships at last are going to experience a great conflict. Our sailors have received the heritage from the marine fusiliers. They envied, they are envied; thus runs the world. If fate destines them to write history with their blood, and no longer merely with their patience, their desire claims the legacy from their brothers who have fallen over there.

End of February.

In one of our trips to carry supplies to Montenegro, the *Dague* has just been lost. In the open roadstead, at midnight, she was waiting for the cargo-boat to finish unloading its bales and cases on the wharf. Her crew was assisting in this dangerous work. The heavy sound of the cases falling on the planks was all that could be heard.... But a submarine from Austria was lying in wait for the *Dague*.

Suddenly the destroyer leaped into the air as if lifted by the hand of a giant. It fell in two pieces like a dead branch of wood. The sailors, enclosed in her sides, did not know they were at the point of death. Thirty seconds later, at the spot where there had been a living ship, and men full of energy, there was no longer anything but the dark water.

1 March.

Malta at last! Landscapes which do not move, roads of hard stone, a desired presence.... Some drives in an English dog-cart behind a frisky pony.... A dress of mauve muslin, the sweet Italian tongue interrupted by silences, the charming visits to the fountain of the swans.

Malta, remote island and jewel of the Mediterranean, blessed repose of navigators, peaceful harbor and immense fortifications, feverish atmosphere and nostalgia of the blue sky. All the roads cross there. Between the antipodes and the fields of battle the Hindu, the Canadians and the French pass several hours there; and later, in the night watches, each one will remember his happy rest in that place.

Malta, the starting point for the warriors of Egypt, of the Dardanelles, of Mesopotamia, and Flanders; the port of call for the sailors of the Mediterranean, of the North Sea and the Persian Gulf. In the Strada Reale clash faces, uniforms, dialects; they linger on the mystical pavements of the churches, and pass into the rocky countryside to dream those dreams one never forgets.

Malta: First pilgrimage of the new crusade. The battleships and cruisers, the drag-nets and dredgers get their second wind here before sailing for the East, for Constantinople. They go there to take part in epic conflicts, and retake from the Osmanlis the city of the Bosphorus, which for five hundred years has awaited its deliverance. Regiments, batteries and squads accompany them, crowded on the transports and eager for victory. May the men who are preparing this great enterprise, this terrible enterprise, measure well its obstacles, and be able to obviate them!

Malta, paradise of the vagabond weary of wandering, light fragrances, exquisite light, enchanting sea, creator of tenderness. Oh, these evenings and mornings when the heart melts in one's breast! But one needs a companion. Woe to the lonely man! He will not appreciate the smiles of this Eden. He cannot enjoy its treasures. How many sailors' wives, who have come here to see for a moment the husbands torn from them seven months ago, will not remember this idyllic spot with tears in their eyes? But other loves are born on this island, which perhaps will die there. These amours I desire every man to have who fights on land or sea. Then a shell will but bring him happiness.

Farewell, Malta! Yesterday under a fragrant arbor the evening light shone on a tragic face, and the coming separation made our speech falter. This morning, towards dawn, in a silent church, two clasped hands and a bowed head were praying for the safety of the traveler. The *Waldeck* left during the day. It took its way slowly among the motionless ships, which will soon sail in their turn. Outside of the harbor, already moving with the swell, it put on full speed and raced over the blue water. Along the ramparts some handkerchiefs and soft hands waved sad farewells. Every one of us, with his glass to his eyes, looked for the beloved face and dress, which were becoming fainter with every turn of the ship's screws. And then distance wiped everything out. Over there lovely eyes have been weeping; here our lids are still wet. The sailor's malady—what is it but separation?

Ionian Sea, 5 March.

The Spring is venturing her first caresses. I know countrysides in France where the cherry trees are already blooming, where violets are fragrant, and lilacs are beginning to unfold. The April sun will soon set flowing the tide of life and bloom; the poppies will get their color from the blood spilled in Champagne and the Vosges.

But upon our sterile sea no grass grows green, no tree blossoms. The water is bluer and the sky paler, the air brings softer breaths, but these beauties are mere phantoms. They glide past like the moments of our monotonous life, like the white clouds filled with light which move above us.

A few living things distract our melancholy. Young porpoises, with silver bellies and slender snouts, play around the hull, lashing the water as if with thongs of whipcord, falling back with a gleaming graceful movement. The old porpoises, mere dignified, follow patiently their continual leapings, sewing the cloth of the sea with an invisible thread; each one of their stitches on this blue material leaves a streak of foam.

When these playful fish pass at a short distance from us, they are amusing. But what frights their more distant tracks through the water have given the officers of the watch! On an empty and shining sea, the silver trail of a porpoise looks too much like the volute of a periscope.... And the periscopes are prowling about.... The fine days have arrived, and the sea is favorable for submarines to come down the Adriatic as far as the Ionian Sea. Many people may not think so, but the cruisers know that the enemy is hunting them to the death. We meet on the water vast flat mirror-like tracks like the trail of a snail on the ground. A submarine has just passed. From one end of the horizon to the other the viscous line is sparkling, but the horizon is empty.

9 March.

Several times at twilight one of the cruisers has seen rising, far away, the kiosk and shell of a submarine, coming to the surface for the night. The cruiser has rushed upon the enemy, but in the splendid evening this fish of steel has filled its reservoirs again and quietly submerged. The red of the sky gives place to purple, and the purple to violet, and the violet to black, to darkness. The cruiser in pursuit has informed the "naval army" of the encounter. We know she is not mistaken, but the other ships, patrolling in the south, treat us as visionaries.

Visionaries indeed! If only we were! We should not then experience, during our watch, these sudden heart failures, and the nights of the watch would not be riddled with these useless agonies. Each day the crews become more apprehensive of some fatal surprise, and no one is indifferent on board except the animals who dwell with us. Happy beasts! Nature has freed them from forebodings.

Our cats, lazy and coquettish, choose a couch on the warm deck in the sun, and roll themselves up in a ball, with their nose resting on their furry paws, their green eyes half closed; or else they stretch out on their sides, stiffening and unbending their paws, and letting the breeze play on their bodies. They forget to sleep. Under the moon or in the darkness they go sidewise, slowly brushing the cordage and the rasping metal. Sometimes they mew with a call that is soft, raucous, and hopeless, for ships of war are chaste, and our poor tomcats spend their nights without any spring amours.

Towards four o'clock in the morning Venus rises fresh and dazzling. Soon the feathery tribe begins to stir. Between the chimneys a cock proclaims his fanfare, the hens cackle, and great disputes, accompanied by much rustling of wings, take place over a cabbage leaf or some water or a grain of corn. Our pigeons coo softly, as they puff their necks; their glossy wings powdered with salt dew. Breaking in on these light sounds comes the lament of the oxen which are to be slaughtered. They low discreetly. At this din, which reminds one of one's native land and one's country home, the officer of the watch on the bridge thinks he smells the odor of the poultry-yard, the healthy odor of dung, and listens to the creaking of the carts as they leave the farm. It is the illusion of homesickness. The only voices of labor are the humming of the ventilators, the pulsation of the engines, and the vibration of the waves which slap the hull. Our only ties with the world are the cruisers, with their stacks and their remote smoke, which go from sector to sector on the same careful vagabondage. And we have no other reason for living than to await the prowling submarines. The submarines, the curse of this war!

11 March.

There is one formidable problem which I have not yet solved.

From the bridge the officer sees a companion vessel explode, sink and disappear. The catastrophe may be slow or swift, it matters not. Many men have just been killed by the explosion; but there remain living survivors in the water, who are condemned to death if their neighbors do not come up to rescue them. The officer's pitiful heart directs him to rush towards the disaster and pick up these brothers of ours.

But no! The submarine is perhaps waiting and is aiming a new torpedo. It is lying in wait for the rescuer with her formidable strength, her thousand able men, and is counting on her rashness to send her to join the victim it has just sunk. The duty of the officer tells him to save a sound ship for France, so that to-morrow she may avenge the dead in some victorious action.

The English Admiralty has solved the dilemma. "Woe to the wounded!" it has said. "I order the living to flee!"

The men who drew up this formidable law in the privacy of their offices were thinking only of the glory of their navy, of the fate of their country. Would these same men, as officers of the watch, hearing the appeal of drowning men, have the terrible courage to flee?

During the long hours of the watch I have pondered over this riddle. To-morrow, this evening, in an instant, the drama of which I am thinking may rise on the horizon. If fate wills that I be struck, I know that as my mouth fills with water, my last cry, to those who approach me will be this:

"Begone, for the submarine is watching for you too!"

But if in the treacherous night or under the kindly sun, I see one of the companion ships of the *Waldeck-Rousseau* destroyed, I hope some inspiration will dictate my conduct. I cannot foresee what it will be. There are tragedies where the reason stumbles, and man is outdone by the malignity of things, where only revelation and divine grace permit him to find his way.

This is the way weariness bewitches one. If we were in action, I should never feel these dilemmas. I should not like to repeat here what all my comrades every minute and every hour are saying around me. Never have the cruisers been plunged into a profounder ennui. The great naval routes pass north or south of our present beats, the battleships are at the Peloponnesus, in Crete, and we can no longer see the coasts of Italy, our companions in recent months. We should never suspect that land existed if wireless messages did not bring us a suggestion of it.

Whence come these birds which for many days now have followed our cruiser as it emerged from the winter? What woods, what nests, have they left? By day they fly from mast to mast, cat-head to bridge, and by night they hide in dark corners.... We are wandering on the treeless waste, two or three hundred kilometers from any shore, and yet these birds with their fragile wings choose our island of steel to rest upon before continuing their journey. They are very young birds, and carry themselves badly upon their inexperienced wings.

14 March.

A swallow, a chaffinch, a robin and a bullfinch, are what I have seen this morning, about sunrise.

In the wide expanse there was the growing light, a pale moon leaning towards the west, some idle curls of smoke, and my vague thoughts. And then, from nowhere, came this chaffinch, and stopped on the bridge at my feet, looked at me impertinently, seemed reassured by its examination, and without further concerning itself with me, began hopping on the floor. Then the swallow arrived, restless and swift, but so awkward that, as it rested on the steel bars, it swayed and caught itself as if it thought it was falling.

It remains faithful to us. The sailors with their affectionate and clumsy hands, have already tied on its dark body a yellow favor which it wears coquettishly. It is our passenger. The others, more lively, only pause between two flights; they peck on our deck, and by chance discover something to store in their tiny paunches; perched on a rod, a partition, or the rigging, they rest awhile, with their heads hunched in their feathers and their wings up to their eyes like blinkers. We call them; they do not answer, for they are asleep. And then all of a sudden the chaffinches and robins fly away, as if they really knew where they were going. They trust themselves without fear to the great mysterious emptiness, and to-morrow other finches and other robins will come, and will also fly away. We love them when they are there. We forget them when they fly away. We shall not weep for their death. They are like us, mariners of the air.

15 March.

They are happier than we, for they are not preoccupied with their fate, all the winds that pass are favorable to their wings. Carelessness is their daily bread. They never ask the reasons for their pilgrimages, and do not guess that their lives might be more useful. We envy their spirit and their empty heads. How many times have we not wished to kill our reason and become like machines, which work without thinking? The sailors cannot know this infinite weariness of anxious thought, and they would never say the bitter things that rise in our minds from the strain of overwork. Are there any combatants in this war who have need of so much patience for so painful a task? For weeks and months, ever since the origin of time, it seems, the sailors have been here performing the same duties, seeing the same faces, hearing the same voices. They know beforehand what their neighbor is going to say. Whether we are paradoxical or bitter, braggart or fatalistic, each of us has long ago finished emptying out his intellectual baggage. There is no chance of evasion or of renewal. One sees the very inside of hearts. Some solid friendships, cemented by common miseries, cheer this existence. But aversions and enmities are strengthened. In many ward rooms now the meals have become gloomy or charged with ill-feeling. One has to keep silent for fear of setting off the evil spark. Everything provides material for discord, and nothing inspires amiable thoughts. One does not wish to make venomous relations that are already strained, and so one says nothing.

Spasmodically, at the reading of an important communiqué or wireless messages, discussions burst forth and wax intense. For the thousandth time we sift over what has been said, and as all the arguments were laid on the table eight months ago, no one can win in the encounter unless he can shout louder than the others. The president of the mess, cool and benevolent, throws himself into the fray, and his advice makes us see the inanity of such disputes. The officers understand that he is right. Better to keep out of it.

Silence falls again. While awaiting his watch, the officer returns to his cabin and tries to forget his troubles. Shall he write to his dear ones? What for, and what shall he say to them? Everyone devotes himself to some mechanical task. This one is learning Spanish, Greek, Japanese; others are measuring their strength on the Ethics of Spinoza, or the theory of the equations of partial derivatives; some are doing carving, collecting stamps or raising turtles. The essential thing is to get a man's mind away from the ship, from the water, from himself.

The night, solitary, kindly, ends with the dawn. Sleep effaces everything, and our duty transforms us into automatons. On the bridge the officer no longer thinks of anything but his superior duties. Near him stand watching the accustomed statues of gunners and steersmen; under him gently vibrates the moving vessel; and all around stretch the silent shadows. Above his head wings like felt open and close, and form rings of sound. They are the horned owls, migratory birds too, which have substituted our masts for their native nests. Frightened, they wheel above the watchers, and their hairy wings sometimes brush our caps. In the blackness of the sky, they fly uncertainly about, hiding the stars and then disclosing them again. Their flight and their silence are congenial to our thoughts. For them the sun does not exist, any more than happiness exists for us. Perhaps they would like the light, but their blinking eyes cannot endure it. They are like our own hearts. For months past we have lost all the joys of life, and dare no longer look them in the face.

17 March.

After four hours of anxious thought and watching, the officer leaves his successor in charge and goes down to his cabin or the ward-room. He is too wide awake to fall quickly asleep, too tired to think. The cruiser is like a castle of the Sleeping Beauty. In the labyrinth of ladders, doors and passages, black holes alternate with the shadows from dim lamps. On each side of the corridors are the rows of closed doors leading to the cabins where the officers and the boatswains toss between insomnia and bad dreams. A smoky light reveals the suspended hammocks. After their hard work the sailors fling themselves down there and sleep just as they fall; their dangling hands and knees are covered with coaldust; many of the faces seem masked in black.

At the staircase to the engine-room, the fireman and swabbers (soutiers) tumble out pell-mell on the metal floor, too exhausted to lift themselves into their hammocks. One has to be careful not to step on someone's chest or ear. The ship could go down, and these men would not wake from their stupor. Some of the more fastidious ones have taken the trouble to procure a pillow; it is a lump of coal, very hard and dusty; their cheeks press it as softly as if it were of down.

With outstretched hands and hesitating feet, the officer makes his round, runs into something, and stops. He passes the watchers, the gunners, the sentries. Wrapped in his cloak, and leaning against the breech, a pointer is observing the flight of the gray water through a port hole. His eyes are wide open, but what can be the reveries of this man who every day and night for so many months has watched the gliding of the water?

"Well, Kersullec, it's tiresome! You are almost through!" whispers the officer.

"Yes, Captain. It isn't that I'm not sleepy, but I'll hold out the rest of my fifty minutes."

And further on:

"You've got your eyes open, eh, Le Bihan? You know that yesterday evening they signaled a submarine.... Quite near...."

"Let it come, Captain. It will see if Le Bihan sleeps on his watch!"

Reaching the ward-room, the officer takes off his cloak, his muffler, his gloves, and puts down his glasses. He nibbles a crust of bread or refreshes himself with a drop of wine. The room is in disorder from the preceding evening, with newspapers left on the red sofas, games on the green tables. One turns the pages mechanically without reading, and shuffles the dominoes and cards without thinking, and before going back to his dull bed, one casts a glance at the betting-book.

22 March.

A happy find, this betting-book, which has banished acrimonious disputes from the *Waldeck-Rousseau*! For since in this war our prophecies about tomorrow or next week have nothing to base themselves upon, what good does it do to argue? If one of us, through some revelation, acquires a definite opinion on future events, he writes it in this notebook with the date, the hour and the place. The page is divided into two columns, one for, and the other against the prediction; the man who bets proposes the stake. The other signs in the right column or the left, and when the bet falls due, the bad prophets pay up as gracefully as possible. There is no opportunity for contradicting, and it is much more amusing than all the discussions.

30 March.

This morning, towards four o'clock, I signed my name in the column of the most recent bets. Here are the three wagers which interested me:

Friday, March 26. 8.50 A.M. at 38° 11′ N. and 16° 11′ E.

M. X.... bets that within three months Italy will be at war, but not Roumania. Stakes a dinner in Paris in 1917, for which the winner shall choose the restaurant and make up the menu.

The page of this wager is scribbled over with emendations and remarks. The number of signatures in the two columns is equal. The winners will be awkward in their triumph.

Sunday, March 28. Midnight: at 38° 02′ N. and 18° 7′ E. M. J.... bets with M. Z.... that the Viviani ministry will not last out the year 1915. Stakes: the two bettors being unmarried, the loser agrees to act as groomsman at the marriage of the winner, who agrees to choose him a pretty maid of honor.

The page is sprinkled with facetious comments. To tell the truth, I do not know which are wittier, those which mention the wager, or those which discuss the stakes. Between the fiancée and the Premier, the maid of honor, the winner and the loser, it is all humor of the cleverest kind.

Tuesday, March 30. 2.30 A.M. at 38° 10′ N. and 16° 23′ E. M. W.... wagers that inside of a month one of the seven Ionian cruisers will be sunk by a submarine and lost without anything's being saved.

For this wager I see neither any stake nor opposing signature.

4 April.

For seven weeks I have not been off the cruiser, but this morning I was given a new duty; namely, to land during our coaling; my turn has come to provide the food for my twenty-five comrades of the mess.

At no time is this a pleasant business; during our war campaign it requires an angelic patience, for supplies are difficult to get and the quality uncertain. Each one of us watches without enthusiasm the day approach when he becomes the scapegoat for the dyspeptics and those with ailing livers. But the implacable schedule, drawn up by lot before our departure from Toulon, appoints a new "chief of the mess" every two months.

You housekeepers who complain of the price of provisions and the bad quality of the eggs had better take passage on the ships which move in the Ionian Sea, and you will learn about unknown miseries. It is no mere question in our latitudes, of varying the menus, of serving such a fish or such a meat, nor even of calculating almost to a half pound what will feed the household without waste. The task is more difficult.

For fifteen or twenty days the cruiser has kept to sea without quitting it; she has done her coaling outside and has not revictualed anywhere. Fresh provisions are a mere memory; eggs, preserved in straw or lime, acquire with each meal a richer and more vigorous flavor. The wine, shaken about in warm casks, ferments. The fresh water absorbs the rust of the iron-casks, and tastes like the mephitic beverage of some invalid resort. Our bread is heavy and indigestible, for the bakers are seasick and the flour is mouldy. For dessert we nibble some empty or frost-bitten walnuts, dried raisins, excessively dried, and almonds which either cannot be cracked or are filled with powder.

Despite our work and weariness, we push aside these pitiful refreshments sweetened with coaldust. Our teeth crack lumps which have no taste of vanilla; these are cinders which have got into our sauces. Morning and evening we have to face one or two dishes of beef. And such beef! Battered by the wind and spray, tossed by the rolling of the ship which bruises their tender nostrils, the poor animals of the shambles trample listlessly the steel deck and sniff their fermented hay listlessly. After a few days at sea they have lost their fat. They have to be killed in time, for fear they will die during the night. For this maritime agony they avenge themselves upon our teeth; their flesh is like a ball of discolored twine, with the pleasant elasticity of rubber. I will not describe the chickens which survive a few weeks of the cruise. I should need the vocabulary of a cordwainer.

And then, in their distant campaignings, the sailors habitually provide themselves with some digestive or rheumatic complaint, which is quiet enough in hours of prosperity, and revives exactly at the moment when one wants to keep well. Seven entire months at sea under this régime have resurrected all these ailments. The martyrs require a light but nourishing diet of good food. Where can we get it? The chief of the mess cannot transform into fresh eggs these shells in which are stirring chicks anxious to hatch out, nor into fresh milk the viscous compound which comes in metal cans. Musty cakes, greenish purées, coagulated rice, become more and more common on our plates. Complexions become yellow, features drawn, and good-humor vanishes. Discussions on the war or the service turn bitter. Those who are endowed with unbroken health take the diatribes philosophically: "Take it easy, my poor friend," they think. "Take it easy. I would reply to you, if it wasn't only your enteritis that is speaking!"

One night a wireless arrives from the Commander-in-Chief.

"You will coal Wednesday at Dragamesti, with the cargo-boat *Marguerite*." It is only Sunday, but a smile appears on a thousand faces. The whole cruiser takes on the alert pace of a horse which sniffs the relay. A sorry relay however! From morning to evening, in a harbor where the wind blows violently, the ship will be shrouded in coaldust; the sailors will wear themselves out, the officers shout themselves hoarse trying to hurry the filling of the sacks, and we shall leave more exhausted than at dawn, for fifteen or twenty days of pilgrimage. But we shall have made a halt. Sailors in any part of the world, you will all understand me!

The chief of the mess is happy, but becomes anxious. Between two watches he has a conference with the cook and steward. Both are neurasthenic; it is as disagreeable to them to prepare our little meals as it is to us to swallow them. But hope, invincible in the heart of man, cheers the trio:

"Captain," says the steward, "buy some figs, some salad and some fresh cheese. That will improve the menu for a week."

"Certainly," replies the captain chief of the mess. "But shall we find any?"

"I want some lambs," demands the cook, "some fish for two or three days, and if I can lay my hand on a good fat sheep, I can guarantee that you gentlemen will be satisfied."

"All right. But I'm afraid we shall not find very much."

"And then, I must have at least four hundred dozen eggs. The last time we only took two hundred; a good half of them were rotten, and we use six to seven dozen a day. So, in twenty days...."

"Oh! But, great heavens, my friend! Where am I to get the money?"

For it is a fact: in war times, and in almost impossible regions, the sailors have for their pay and food not a cent more than in times of peace. Upon this detail the chief of the mess has his own opinion, but keeps it to himself. Pencil and memorandum in hand, he wavers between fear of overspending his credit, and of incurring the anathema of his comrades. He opens his till and counts the notes and change, closes the lock with a sharp click and murmurs:

"I shall never get away with it...."

Monday and Tuesday pass. The general satisfaction increases. The furrows deepen on the brow of the chief of the mess. To-morrow is Wednesday, the fatal day. But at dusk another wireless message arrives:

"Collier *Marguerite* delayed by bad weather. You will coal Thursday with the *Circe*."

At this delay which desolates all the others, the chief of the mess calms down and has a better sleep. He has just gained twenty-four hours. But his calm is shaken at table by the remarks which unanimously agree that the food is uneatable—they are right—and that the chief of the mess ought to be hung. Poor chief of the mess!

A third wireless follows:

"Remain in the third sector until next Saturday. You will coal Sunday at Santa Maura with the *Bayonnais*."

Horror and desolation! The language of sailors is not unresourceful, but in desperate cases it becomes magnificent. This is one of them. Rabelais himself, the prince of truculence, would open his ears wide to hear the sailors—ordinarily civilized—comment on this third message. I dare not reproduce these explosions, but will keep to my hero, the chief of the mess.

The bitterest pleasantries have an end. Towards sunrise the ship finds its way to the appointed rendezvous and anchors there. I will not say it is at Santa Maura, or on Sunday, or with the *Bayonnais*. It may be with the *Biarritz*, at Antipaxo, on the following Wednesday. We are within neither a week or a hundred kilometers of the original order, but the cruiser lies still, with the collier alongside, and the crew have already plunged into a cyclone of black dust. With his pocket full, but with an anxious heart, the chief of the mess, accompanied by his two acolytes, reaches the shore in a steam cutter. There is nothing but ten houses and a small church. The horizon consists of solid rock, without a sign of cultivation. At each step the hope of provender diminishes. We touch the quay, if there is a quay; when there is nothing better we run up on the beach, and the trio makes for the cluster of houses. Some Greeks with intelligent smiles and unintelligible language are always to be found to conduct you to persons who will sell you eggs, poultry, groceries or animals. They take your hand and pull you by the sleeve. They show certificates from another cruiser which has left the evening before, and which, like the brigand she is, has surely taken everything! After many muddy puddles, many ruts, the three victims arrive in front of the herd, the poultry-yard, or the baskets of fruit.

I suspect the people of this region of having founded along their coasts sanatoriums of lymphatic sheep and tuberculous cattle. I suspect them of cultivating boxwood and fusain, cutting the twigs off with scissors, and calling them salad. I suspect them finally when they sell eggs at eight sous apiece, of wishing to give you your money's worth, and of setting odor above cheapness.

"If you want to see better animals, there is another herd ten kilometers away, behind the marshes."

"In that island opposite, I know a man who grows vegetables; go to him. It will only take you three hours there and back."

"Yes, you could find fresher eggs at my neighbor's, but he just left for the mountains last night."

The chief of the mess devotes forty minutes to understanding these wily proposals. He has only a few hours in this remote region, and before night he has to provide for the food of twenty-five men for twenty days. Followed by the steward and the cook, he perspiringly visits the miserable shops and doubtful poultry-yards.

"We have no more figs or raisins. The Germans bought them all three months ago."

"Yesterday one of your ships took the finest head of cattle. If you had only come the day before yesterday!"

Hours pass, but they do not in the least improve the quality of what we are offered. The agents become more and more cunning as they press you to buy, for they know that the cruiser sails at dusk, and their kind souls fear she will leave without provisions. In a creaking carriage or on a broken horse, the chief of the mess goes to see this herd, or that famous poulterer, and returns with a desire to slaughter his guide. Evening comes. The cruiser whistles, raises the flag of recall, and is to put to sea in half an hour. We must buy now, whatever the cost. Then pell-mell, in sacks or boxes, under the goad of the shepherds, on the shoulders of the boys, the eggs and suspect vegetables, the consumptive animals and the parchment poultry begin to move towards the cutter. The Chief's spirit is haunted by dark presentiments, but he offers fresh blue notes and new gold pieces in exchange for these precarious victuals. The sons of Mercury wrangle over the change and the price, the porters demand their tip, and the market becomes an uproar of invective. But all that is nothing to what is in store on board.

At last everything is in order. The cutter leaves the quay, followed by pleasantries, and arrives at the ship, which weighs anchor and begins in the night its twenty days of cruising. In answer to the questions of his comrades the chief of the mess tries to put on a good face, but the evening meal gives him a hint of the refined torture he will endure until the next landing, and he invokes the god of resignation to his aid.

This afternoon, since I had used up my store of gold and silver, I gave a hundred franc note to some breeder of elastic chickens. I owed him fourteen francs. Instead of giving me back eighty-six francs, he made the entire change for the note in pieces of five, two and one drachmas. In the midst of a crowd of boys and attentive men he counted it, recounted it, and put it in my hand.

From these hundred francs which he gave me I took out two five-drachma pieces and two two-drachma pieces, making up the total amount. But he returned me the two five-drachma pieces, and I cannot describe the air with which he said to me: "Your two coins are bad. Give me two others."

If I had been a German, I should have knocked him on the head. But I contented myself with throwing the two coins into a pile of mud that happened to be there, and jumped into my cutter without saying a word. As we returned, I examined the other coins. They were sound. And I could not help laughing, for if I had chosen two good coins to pay him with, this good breeder would have robbed me of ten francs.

I have traveled much, I have seen many swindlers; but this one takes the first prize.

Strait of Otranto,
25 April to 1 May, 1915.

The cruisers on the Ionian Sea have received orders to go up as far as the Strait of Otranto. Perhaps the Commander-in-Chief, who is stationed towards the south of Greece, has learned that the Austrians are preparing certain naval operations and so sends us to watch the enemy at closer range; perhaps this movement corresponds to some play on the chess-board of war. Little do we care. We leave these desert regions, and go to find the friends of our early days: Santa Maria de Leuca, Fano, Corfu.

Again we encounter their charms and their graces. Autumn had decked them in soft colors; April envelops them in a virginal light. At the end of Italy the lighthouse of Leuca rises like a marble finger always white; and the islands and the mountains of Epirus are pink in the morning, blue through the day, and mauve at dusk. The air is so marvelously pure that the night itself does not rob things of their color. Violets and yellows remain, even under the moon.

We have plenty of time to admire these beauties, already so familiar. The cruisers move very slowly, for they must not use too much coal. Several times we have been surprised to find one of them wanting to hurry the schedule of coalings and do its provisioning two or three days earlier. So in order not to incur the reproach of stopping oftener than is necessary, the cruisers have taken a leisurely pace, and the consumption of fuel has become satisfactory. Especially at night, in the religious calm over which the hills of Corfu and the lighthouse of Leuca watch as sentinels, it seems that we are quite motionless.

The family of cruisers, which was formerly dispersed over the Ionian Sea, now meet each other continually, and play at puss in the corner. In the course of a day one sees three or four gently rise on the horizon, make a curve as they double the edge of their sector, and nonchalantly depart again. When they have something to say, two comrades approach each other: the *Ferry* talks to the *Gambetta* by wigwagging, the *Waldeck* to the *Renan* with flags and pennants; through the glass one recognizes friends; salutations are exchanged by waving caps or hands. When the conversations are finished, each one turns her back and goes to patrol her watery field. Every morning, from eight to nine o'clock, the ships signal information about the amount of coal remaining, their daily consumption, the number of sick on board, and the number of the sector they are patrolling. If one of them has done or sighted something interesting, she mentions it. We have a little daily chat; thanks to which we feel less lonely—within reach of a voice, so to speak. During their watch the officers consult the memoranda of the wireless messages, and read hastily the news from their neighbors, just as one listens, without paying attention, to the friend one meets in the street who gives one the bulletin of his family's good health.

We have, moreover, plunged back into the great road of international traffic. Again the throng of steamers, freighters or sailing vessels, passes along the Italian and Greek coasts. We may not go too near them, for fear of penetrating the territorial waters, and of thus finding Italy or Greece, with whom the Entente is carrying on negotiations, touchy about their sea frontiers. If one of the cruisers visits some ship too near the limit, she is accused of having overstepped the line, and the affair, exaggerated, becomes disquieting. Better to evade the controversial line, and only accost, with a clear conscience, the ships that risk themselves on the high sea.

In order that the crews may not lose their skill in firing the guns, which sleep in a profound slumber during this disconcerting war, from time to time we practise firing at floating targets. Not shooting with a regular charge, for our guns make so much noise that an hour later all the telegraphs of the world would announce "the great naval battle in the Strait of Otranto," but what is called in the navy reduced firing. With small charges and small shells we fire upon little canvas targets which float on the water like children's toys driven by the breeze. This makes proportionately no more noise than a pea-shooter firing peas, but the entire organism of the ship—engines, system of direction and of firing, telemetry and rules of firing—functions as it would in battle. When we pick up the target the crew examines the canvas and the framework, counts the holes and the scratches, criticizes this parody of battle. A pitiful solace for our desire for action! One thought consoles us: the Austrians at Pola, the Germans at Kiel, the English in the bases where they wait, are tiring themselves with the same vanities as ourselves, with reduced firing and the pretences of battle. Yes, this naval war is indeed disconcerting.

These were my thoughts during the watch the other night, when everything about me was so fair. A full moon with soft features, but with a contour as sharp as that of a new medal, rode in a sky as pure as the face of a child. The stars were swollen with joy. Vague lightning illuminated first one part of the sky and then another, like vagrant smiles of the night, without arrière-pensée. The sea, drowsy with warmth, had a calm and fragrant breath, and it seemed as if our prow in cutting it was profaning a divine slumber. It was one of those moments when the most unhappy man feels love flood his heart, and as my eyes fell only on eternal things, my spirit absorbed all their blessing. The cruiser was patrolling the middle of the Strait of Otranto; on its left a comrade kept guard towards Fano and Corfu; on its right the *Gambetta* in the Italian sector received from time to time the flashes from the lighthouse. During the afternoon we had come quite near the *Gambetta*; our boats had exchanged the parcels, the mail, and orders, and it is now the *Waldeck-Rousseau* who will occupy the Italian sector after we separate. At the last moment some new order has given our place to the *Gambetta* and kept us in the central rectangle. It is of no particular importance, and our turn to be neighbors with the lighthouse will come to-morrow.

I shall not try to describe the train of thought which haunts the officer of the watch when nature becomes kindly again and accords him a respite for his body. As he surveys the sea with unrelenting eyes, he makes the tour of the weather, of the world, of his ideas. The fluttering butterfly is less capricious than this reverie of his, but he rests at last on some flower of thought. I remember that on this night, towards the third hour of my watch, I was thinking of the contrast between the peace of Nature and the human agony of the war. I had taken off my cap to feel the caressing fingers of the night; I had even opened my vest, and felt almost on my skin the freshness of the reviving breeze. On the sea, so light that it seemed transparent, I saw nothing in particular; but that was undoubtedly the weakness of my vision, the fatigue from too long cruises, the lassitude which on this night all my comrades of the watch on the cruisers felt with me. Otherwise my mind was clear.

The work of France and Russia, the enterprise of the Dardanelles and Gallipoli, all that had not been done, all that could be done, and ought to be done, everything defined itself in precise images. Around the cruiser was so much silence and so much silent light that my thoughts seemed to speak aloud to me. When my successor came to replace me on the watch, I quickly told him all the routine things, and then remained several minutes before going down to my cabin, in order to enjoy the marvelous night for a little while longer. There was not a single sound or light, and I left the bridge regretfully. I thought of the officers of the nearby cruisers, towards the right and the left of us, several miles away, feeling the same sensations, and I was consoled.

The arriving day brought dazzling beauty after the quiet charm of the night, but everything around the cruiser remained the same—calm, silence, warm air. After a heavy sleep, a listless morning and a short meal, I resumed at noon the interrupted watch. The same thoughts continued to accompany my duties. Between them there was only the difference of moonlight and sunlight. My reasonings were clearer, my rancor stronger, but the sparkling of the waves revealed nothing. As we had nothing to communicate to the cruisers on our right and left, we remained quietly in the center of our sector, and my only companions of the watch were the sun, the migrating birds and some dolphins in the water.

Towards two o'clock I received the sudden news of the death of a sailor on board. The news tore me from my peaceful mood. I know that in this far place the death of one man does not count, especially when one is acquainted with that man only by a number. Yet I could not refrain from a certain melancholy, and the train of my reveries became somber. You poor little sailor, who has given up his life in this iron prison, where will be your grave? The perfumed rocks of Greece, or the sands of Apulia, or a shroud in the Ionian deeps? Wherever it be, no hand will ever strew flowers on your white wooden cross, and those who write you to-day perhaps will not know to what part of the vast world they should direct their tears.

To the end of my watch I keep thinking of this destiny of the sailors, who do not even halt to die. Around me the faces of the lookouts and gunners show the same aspect of gravity which mine should have. This morning, it seems to me, touches us more than it should. Is there not going on somewhere a drama much more terrible?

In order to banish such reflections, I go to look in my cabin for my little dog Jimmino, with his cold nose, his soft eyes and silky hair. Since my last stay in Malta, he has exchanged the ease of his mistress' home for the hard existence of a ship. At night he sleeps in the hollow of my shoulder, and when he wakes, he watches my slumber without stirring. When I work, he whines softly until I lift him up on my desk. He puts his head between his paws, and follows the course of my pen. He does not like me to remain too long without speaking to him, for I think he is of a jealous temperament. In order to let me know he is there, Jimmino rises and walks across my pages where his paws trail thick threads of ink. Then I give him a little tap on his cold nose and scold him:

"Get away, you horrible, badly brought up little thing! What would your mother say if she..."

"Well, well," replies the little tail as it wags. "You have spoken, silent master, and you have struck me; so you must love me. I am not vexed with you any more."

Jimmino lies down again within reach of the paper, his nose so near the sheets that at the end of every line I feel his warm breath on the back of my fingers. He watches my bent head, and thinks:

"I know very well you are bored, and that you brought me with you to distract you. I am very happy when you deign to think of me. But do you suppose that I am amused? Formerly, I played with the cat, on the stairs, under the furniture, and around the kitchen. Everything smelt good all around, and they washed me every morning. Here everything is full of coal and bad odors. The moving sea makes me dizzy. And then I have become the dog of an officer, and cannot go with the crews' pets. What have I done that you should exile me? Listen to me, silent master. Speak to me."

The paw stretches out cautiously to the edge of my freshly written line. "Back, Jimmino! You will make a bad blot!"

The paw draws back.

"Bah! You are right," the master goes on. "It is late. In a quarter of an hour we shall eat. Come up on the bridge. We will take the air."

I take Jimmino, warm and soft, up on my shoulder, where he weighs nothing. He settles himself, snuggles against my ear which he tickles. He trembles at my rapid course along the corridors, up the companion ways, to the height of the bridge.

The twilight is marvelous with its soft and delicate shades of color.

"What news?" I say to the officer of the watch.

"Nothing.... The same old story."

"Any interesting messages?"

"None! Communiqués from Eiffel, Norddeich, Poldhu. The cruisers have nothing to say. Go read the memorandum."

I hasten to read the book of telegrams, glancing over the hundred or two hundred messages of the day. It is the same strain as yesterday, and as it will be to-morrow. "Left Navaria at 2 P.M.," says this one. "I count on finishing coaling this evening," says another. "I am on my way to Bizerta," says a third, and so on for four pages.

"Well," says the officer of the watch. "You see there is nothing."

"It's queer. The *Gambetta* has not spoken to-day."

"There was probably nothing to announce."

"It should have signaled its daily position this morning."

"Wireless damaged perhaps."

"Perhaps. All the same it has said nothing since 9 o'clock last night."

"Have any of the cruisers called her?"

"Yes! And she has not responded."

"You are sure?"

"Go and see. I will watch in your place."

Five minutes later my comrade returns, after running over, examining and considering the four pages of messages.

"You are right," he says. "It is strange. However, nothing has happened to her. She would always have had time to signal S. O. S. That doesn't take two seconds."

"That's true. But all the same, she should have replied to the ships that called her."

"She was wrong. We shall see to-morrow."

I go down to dinner. On my chair Jimmino, crouched like a sphinx, is waiting for bits from my meal. Our assembly is not very noisy. We comment upon the end of the day, and the doctor receives placidly the usual pleasantries. The conversation turns listlessly on Turkish affairs. Why is there no animation? The officers who are going to take the watch rise to put on their uniforms for the night. We greet them in the familiar way as they pass out. "A good watch to you, old man! Keep your eyes open!" "Don't delay us!" "You know I'm taking the Paris express this evening." "If you see a submarine try not to waken me." "And then," I added, "let me know if there is a message from the *Gambetta*."

"Why?"

"She has not spoken for nearly twenty-four hours."

"The deuce!" murmured the assembly. "What has happened to her?"

The game tables are set up, for dominoes, chess, bridge; the smokers light their pipes; the readers open their paper; others stretch out on the cushions. Interpretations are offered concerning the silence of the *Gambetta*.

"Accident to the wireless...."

"She had nothing to say...."

"She ought to have signaled her daily position...."

"She should have replied when she was called...."

"We shall see to-morrow...!"

The cards fall, the dominoes grate, the newspapers crackle, and the pipes pull. All in this little world are silent, absorbed in their game, their reading or their reveries. But it is appearance only. Yesterday afternoon we talked with the *Gambetta*; last night she cruised in the sector where we were to go. For twenty-four hours she has been silent. In the cards, in the papers, and the smoke from the pipes, each one of us reads these disquieting thoughts. But no one speaks of it. I go to bed, for I have to take the watch again in the middle of the night.

Jimmino trots behind me, installs himself near the pillow, and sleeps with a dreamless slumber. But I await through the long hours some news of the *Gambetta*. Eyes closed or open, I cannot escape being haunted by her. All my comrades tell me they have passed a sleepless night.

In the shadow I go up to take the watch. My predecessor repeats the sacred phrases. I interrupt him:

"But the *Gambetta*?"

"Nothing."

"What do you think of it?"

"Nothing."

"Do you believe that...?"

I dare not finish. He dares not answer, but disappears in the darkness.

I fix my eyes on this treacherous sea which never gives up its secrets. An anguish with iron fingers presses my heart. There is no more doubt of it, death has passed over one of our brothers. Each hour that slips by proves the magnitude of the disaster, and if no news ever reaches us, it will be because all at one stroke eight hundred men will have plunged into the sea. Leaning on the rail, I stroke the metal mechanically, and the wood and canvas which meet my hand. I enjoy feeling the good cruiser, alive and in motion, quivering under me. I realize how much I love her, and it seems to me, that in order to pierce the darkness, my eyes take on the acuteness of a father's who scans the face of a child of his that is menaced by death.

A little later our wireless operator sends me a bundle of messages. With nervous fingers the ensign translator turns over his codes and dictionaries in order to transform these ciphers into French. Each minute I go to his shoulder to read the line, or the half-line, or the word he has transcribed. Heavens! How long it takes to spell out the horror!

It happened yesterday evening, during that fatal watch which I found so beautiful. The moon was quite round; the sea was transparent, and I saw nothing on it. Like me the officers on watch on the *Gambetta* were weary of their useless vigil; at the end of their route they saw the gleam of the lighthouse at Santa Maria di Leuca. In the distance passed the shadows which I should have seen if the *Waldeck-Rousseau* had cruised in the sector which it was to have had. These shadows were ships going along the Italian coast.

But another shadow, covered by the water, had been on watch for many days. It knew we were going by way of the Strait of Otranto. Advised by its accomplices, it awaited, motionless, the occasion for striking a decisive blow. For three nights, for four nights, the majestic cruisers passed too far from this shadow submarine, from this octopus with deadly tentacles. The moon, as it approached its full glory, became more and more luminous.

During these splendid hours, when I had almost disrobed to feel the caresses of the night near me, the submarine saw approaching a slowly moving vessel, with four stacks and graceful outline. It made ready, as it had the night before and the night before that, and hoped that the ship's present route would permit it to cast its death thrust.

What pen could describe this drama in all its fullness?

On the *Gambetta*, sailors and officers scanned this sea that was almost too bright; they had seen it raging or seething with billows, or tormented by the wind, or calmer than a sleeping eyelid. It was the ninth month! Flashes of lightning dazzled their eyes, and they moved, like the watchers on the *Waldeck-Rousseau*, in a confusion of gleams and darkness. It was the two hundredth night! They were weary. They had waited so long, they no longer expected anything. Their eyes met only illusion.

The submarine lay in wait in the bosom of the waves. It knew that some time or other its wonderful prey would pass within range of its torpedo. Through the lens of the periscope its commander saw the luminous circle where the moon danced, the surface of the mirrored water, and the phantoms which move in a night at sea. He heard on the submerged hull the lapping of the dark waves. All the sailors at their posts watched the gesture of his hand and the sound of his voice.

Suddenly this man's heart began to beat as if it would burst. God of death, you were speaking in his ear! He had just seen in the funnel of his periscope two masts and four stacks. She rose in the midst of the lightning flashes, a phantom. Tense and still, the man asked himself if the vision would approach, or would vanish as on the preceding nights. She approached. She came, a vagabond, predestined, without knowing that a demon was plotting her death. With closed lips and moist hands, this man prepared his words. Twenty-five men watched him as if he were a destroying angel.

At the given moment he said: "Fire!"

The torpedo left the submarine like a breath in the water and as silently. For a few seconds, a few endless seconds, it rushed through the echoless water. Two flashes, three flashes, gleamed in the sky; the lookouts on the *Gambetta* covered their faces with their hands. They did not suspect that this moment, which followed so many other moments, held in it the last breath they would draw.

Then a dull sound behind her made the cruiser tremble. She was seized with a sudden fever, and each of her metal plates resounded. Death spread through her limbs and muscles. In through a breach in her very heart rushed the dark water, leaped and broke everything before it. What happened then?

I do not know. I do not yet know. But some of the messages make it possible to imagine the details of the horror.

Filled with water on her wounded side, the *Gambetta*, lurched toward her sea grave, and the sailors who were not killed at once thrust out their arms to save themselves. Everything slid around them. To stand upright they had to lean over; their hands had to serve them for eyes, for darkness enveloped the cruiser. Naked and silent they rushed on toward the deck, but the slanting companion ways were now as perpendicular as walls. How many unfortunates perished in their suddenly interrupted sleep, without realizing that their ship was going down for the last time?

On the deck, a black chaos! Each second the cruiser sinks deeper. The gulf of the waves grows larger, and each moment perhaps will be the final plunge. By main force the sailors launch the boats and the cutter, which drop into the water wrong side or right side up. The officers are calm and have put aside their fatigue; they give the necessary orders for the rescue. In the sky the two masts and the four stacks sink lower and lower. The cruiser, with its apparatus damaged, can send out no signal for help, and all those who dwell on her plunge into the depths as if down a silent stair.

A handful of men have been able to enter the boats. Chilled, but struggling for life, they have taken the oars, and during the last hours of the night have rowed towards the friendly lighthouse. At the first gleam of day, with bleeding hands, but with a marvelous tenacity of will, they have made a supreme effort, and the Italian customs-officers take in sixty exhausted men almost at the point of death.

From Tarentum to Rome, from Rome to Paris, from Paris to Malta, and from Malta to the *Waldeck-Rousseau*, this story of the drama has been traveling for twenty-four hours. The good neighbor we loved to see in our meetings on the high sea has met the death which might have been our own. She has disappeared without a word, felled at the first stroke in an eddy of the sea, as befalls her pilgrims. The wound was muffled and dumb, for over there on the horizon I saw nothing. One of the flashes that played in the sky was perhaps the gleam of the torpedo which killed her, but I was deceived by the illusion of distance.

Without mourning or benediction they laid their bodies in the cemetery of the sea. From Admiral to midshipmen, all the officers are buried in this sea, at once so maternal and malevolent. The superhuman souls of these officers attempted the impossible. They wished to save the cruiser, and the cruiser went down. They wished to save the men, and it is not their fault that nearly eight hundred sailors perished.

And then, according to that law of the sea which ordains that the officer shall wait until the last sailor is saved, they went down with their ship. The ignorant will criticize them, but they are wrong. If each Frenchman, in civil or military service, performs to the uttermost the task his country demands of him, his country, with a heave of her shoulders, will chase the Germans out of France.

Officers of the *Gambetta*, you have your place in the paradise of "*la Revanche.*"

FINIS.

Milton Keynes UK
Ingram Content Group UK Ltd.
UKHW030741071024
449371UK00006B/648